BELIEF
AND
SCIENCE

Joe Walker

Cartoons by Moira Munro

HODDER
GIBSON
AN HACHETTE UK COMPANY

The Publishers would like to thank the following for permission to reproduce copyright material:

Page 1 © Ingram Publishing Limited; page 4 © Vikram Raghuvanshi/iStockphoto.com; page 5 © Photodisc/Getty Images; page 14 © Chris Balcombe/Rex Features (foreground) and Hodder Faith; page 18 © Ingram Publishing Limited; page 21 © Jeff J Mitchell/Getty Images; page 22 (left) © Getty Images/ Digital Vision, (right) © Kippa Matthews/Rex Features; page 27 © AfriPics.com/Alamy; page 34 © Ashley Cooper/Corbis; page 38 © Digital Vision/Getty Images; page 41 © Volodymyr Kyrylyuk/ iStockphoto.com; page 43 © Jupiter Images/Creatas/Alamy; page 45 © Phototake Inc./Alamy; page 49 © Tim Bradley/ Stone/Getty Images; page 55 © akg-images/Erich Lessing; page 58 © Jeremy Sutton Hibbert/Rex Features; page 60 © AP Photo/Christophe Simon, pool/Press Association Images; page 62 © CBS/Everett/Rex Features; page 64 © Sipa Press/ Rex Features; page 66 © amana images inc./Alamy; page 68 (top) © Thom Lang/Corbis, (bottom) © Christopher Furlong/Getty Images; page 81 © Jim Zuckerman/Corbis; page 94 © NASA/ STScI/Rice Univ./C.O'Dell et al.; page 97 © NASA; page 98 © Bettmann/CORBIS; page 99 © COBE Project [http://lambda. gsfc.nasa.gov/product/cobe/], DMR [http://lambda.gsfc.nasa.gov/ product/cobe/ dmr_overview.cfm], NASA [http://www.nasa.gov/ home/index.html]; page 112 © akg-images/Erich Lessing; page 113 © Johnny Van Haeften Ltd., London/ The Bridgeman Art Library; page 118 © Anne Katrin Purkiss/Rex Features; page 129 © Bibliotheque Nationale, Paris, France/The Bridgeman Art Library; page 131 © Sipa Press/Rex Features; page 133 © akg-images/Erich Lessing; page 136 © Imagestate Media; page 140 © Pedro Ugarte/AFP/Getty Images; page 141 © akg-images; page 142 © akg-images/Erich Lessing; page 146 (top) © Sipa Press/Rex Features, (bottom) © Jewel Samad/ AFP/Getty Images; page 152 (top) © Science Photo Library, (bottom) © Javier Trueba/MSF/Science Photo Library; page 153 (top) © George Bernard/NHPA, (bottom) © Andrew Querner/ Aurora Creative/Getty Images; page 154 (top) © Peggy Greb/US Department of Agriculture/Science Photo Library, (bottom) © Paul Souders/Corbis; page 155 (top) © The Natural History Museum/Alamy, (bottom) © Wellcome Library, London; page 156 © Wellcome Library, London; page 157 © Owen Franken/Corbis; page 159 © Bettmann/Corbis; page 161 © Photodisc/Getty Images; page 165 © Universal Images Group Limited/Alamy; page 177 © Roger Ressmeyer/Corbis.

Running heads: Chapters 1 and 11 © Jill Fromer/iStockphoto.com; Chapters 2, 3 and 4 © Sebastian Meckelmann/iStockphoto.com; Chapters 5, 6 and 7 © Digital Vision/Getty Images; Chapters 8, 9 and 10 © iStockphoto.com.

Acknowledgements
The author would like to thank Lorna and David again for their support and encouragement throughout this writing process and all the others. Thanks too are due in no small part to John Mitchell and Katherine Bennett at Hodder Gibson for their support, advice and encouragement over the years. Particular thanks are due to them this time for their patience while waiting for this manuscript, which was somewhat delayed by the author's involvement in something called A Curriculum for Excellence… (Thanks to the many colleagues who gave their support while I tried to navigate that little minefield…) Thanks also to Nadia Cowan, PT RMPS, for initial prodding to get on with this book. Thanks also to Ian Thow, setter for the SQA in the Belief and Science Unit, and David Jack, Principal Assessor for AH RMPS. Thanks also to Adelle Fleming, PT RMPI at Gracemount High School, for further checks on the scientific elements and to Kirsty Newlands for helping to assess readability. Thanks to Graham Crawford, PT Science at Liberton High School, for talking through the Big Bang theory and for encouraging the author to play backing sax on a Japanese rock band's CD (strange but true…) As ever, any errors are mine alone and I'll be happy to put them right in the 2nd printing, but would have to have a sell-out of the first print first.

Although every effort has been made to ensure that website addresses are correct at time of going to press, Hodder Gibson cannot be held responsible for the content of any website mentioned in this book. It is sometimes possible to find a relocated web page by typing in the address of the home page for a website in the URL window of your browser.

Hachette's policy is to use papers that are natural, renewable and recyclable products and made from wood grown in sustainable forests. The logging and manufacturing processes are expected to conform to the environmental regulations of the country of origin.

Orders: please contact Bookpoint Ltd, 130 Milton Park, Abingdon, Oxon OX14 4SB. Telephone: (44) 01235 827720. Fax: (44) 01235 400454. Lines are open 9.00 – 5.00, Monday to Saturday, with a 24-hour message answering service. Visit our website at www.hoddereducation.co.uk. Hodder Gibson can be contacted direct on: Tel: 0141 848 1609; Fax: 0141 889 6315; email: hoddergibson@hodder.co.uk

© Joe Walker 2009
First published in 2009 by
Hodder Gibson, an imprint of Hodder Education,
An Hachette UK Company,
2a Christie Street
Paisley PA1 1NB

Impression number 5 4 3 2 1
Year 2013 2012 2011 2010 2009

Cover photo Coneyl Jay/Science Photo Library
Illustrations by Moira Munro
Typeset in Garamond 12pt by DC Graphic Design Limited, Swanley Village, Kent
Printed in Italy

A catalogue record for this title is available from the British Library

ISBN-13: 978 0340 973 028

Contents

CHAPTER 1

Christianity and Science in the 21st Century

Look at the world around you. Marvel at the variety of life on Planet Earth, be awe-inspired by the size and complexity of the Universe as you stare at the starry skies on a clear night. Remind yourself that your life is unique, that the microscopic DNA which is the pattern for you is a unique product of the wonderful thing that is life. Just think about the planet upon which you live – where pretty much every conceivable space is filled with teeming life forms – even the air you are breathing right now. Think about the delicate balance of life on Earth, how if it were just a little bit different then there might be no life at all, or at least no life that we would recognise. Think about the fact that you are sitting there thinking, consciously able to reflect upon your life and your place in the Universe, as will your children and their children for generations to come.

Now think about the things humans can do – the diseases we have brought to an end, the life-saving technologies which can do so much good. Think also of the things we cannot yet do, and the journey we still have to make to bring our world into a state where justice and freedom, to name but two, are commonplace. Now think outwards to other worlds, the stars and black holes and the vast emptiness of space and the occasional planet, perhaps like ours, perhaps also teeming with life. Consider the unimaginable size of the Universe and the incredible power of the forces within it. Consider that the light from those stars you see has landed on the retina at the back of your eye, having travelled through space for millions of years at the speed of light itself. Think of the power and size of those stars that they have the energy to make this possible – to let you see today something which started its journey many aeons ago. Think of our own human species, so fragile and yet so powerful. The species which dominates our home-world today, but whose life could be brought to an end through a simple cosmic accident or through its own stupidity...

Now think of the possible explanations for many of these things: that humans are simply the latest in the line of life on Earth... beings in a tiny unremarkable planet in a miniscule little galaxy... beings that have existed as a species for only the blink of an eye in the cosmic timescale... and beings who may well disappear just as quickly, to be replaced by something else entirely, never to be remembered. Or more positively, a life form which has developed in such a way that it is the Universe's first and only way of being conscious of itself. Or, alternatively, beings created by the creator of all things – a being itself, existing outside of space and time, which made everything there is, and has a special place in some great plan for our seemingly insignificant little species. Think of the role of this species as either just another form of life (no different to any other that has been or ever will be) or as something quite remarkable – a species with a mighty role to play in the unfolding of the Universe. Perhaps, in fact, the Universe's only such life form.

Throughout the history of life on Earth, humans have probably always had a sense of wonder about the world around them – a sense of awe, but also a fear of the great powers of nature. Humans have probably always asked questions about their place in it all, from looking at the rise of the sun and asking how it comes to disappear and reappear each day, to looking at themselves and questioning their purpose in what seems such a short life. Humans have speculated on answers to these questions and those answers have probably fallen into at least two categories: those which could be called 'religious' answers and those which are 'scientific'. Some people have always seen these as opposites, and some have seen them as complementary. Some think you cannot be religious and accept scientific explanations for life's 'big questions' and others think the opposite.

The history of the interaction between religion and science is complex. For much of the history of humanity, 'power' in society was wielded by those who were believed to have 'special access' to the gods – the shamans and holy men and women who called down the spirits to heal or to harm and who bathed in the light of their special power, which came from their ability to communicate with the gods themselves. Throughout human development, the power of these holy men and women has been challenged (some might say destroyed) by the rise of a scientific approach to life – where our interaction with nature and its powerful forces became something to be understood and worked with, rather than something to be pacified and bowed down to. For example, in many civilisations, the relationship between the gods and the seasons was a close one. The priests or royals kept the gods happy and in return the gods blessed them with the food they needed to survive. When the crops failed, it was believed that the gods had been angered and so had to be made happy again – through sacrifices – sometimes of the priests or royals themselves. Then everything would return to normal. However, as time went on, some would try things out and test the beliefs of the day, perhaps by trying to cure illness through practical means instead of 'spiritual' ones, or ensuring crop growth through irrigation schemes rather than ritual sacrifice.

Gradually, some people became more attracted to these practical responses to living than they were to the spiritual ones. And so a division of sorts grew up between those who interacted with the world through scientific means and those who did so through religious ones. Eventually, as is the case today, some would come to believe that the only way to understand the world around them was through science and others believed that the only way was through religion. Of course there were some, as there still are and may always be, who see the world through both sets of eyes – finding no conflict between science and religion which they cannot resolve. In the western world, the dominant religious force for the moment remains Christianity and the dominant scientific force the science which follows the principles of the modern scientific method. Can they live together or are they opposites in a battle which must eventually see a winner emerge? That is the subject of this book and all of the topics and questions it explores will try to come to some conclusions about these. The topics are complex and the evidence and viewpoints supporting (and opposing) them are equally complex. However, this search for 'meaning, value and purpose' in life is fundamental to human nature and this search can lead to religious conclusions, scientific ones, or mixtures of the two. In short, this book will explore the views of those who think that:

◆ Religion is wrong in its methods and assumptions and therefore in the way that it views life, the Universe and everything.

◆ Science is wrong in its methods and assumptions and therefore in the way that it views life, the Universe and everything.

◆ Science and religion are both partly right in their assumptions and therefore in the way that they understand life, the Universe and everything.

In particular, this book will explore the relationship between the Christian faith and modern science. There are responses to all of the scientific issues you will consider from other faiths, of course, but these aren't in the SQA course at the moment. The relationship between Christianity and modern science will be explored by examining:

◆ their methods of arriving at human understanding (Area 1)

◆ their views about the origins of the Universe (Area 2)

◆ their views about the origin and development of human life (Area 3).

Christianity in the 21st Century

Depending upon who you ask, Christianity is either a relic from a superstitious past or something which still gives meaning and purpose to people's lives all over the world. Christianity is the largest single religion in the world today, and exists in pretty much every country in the world. There are many facts and figures about Christianity, but as they are constantly changing there's little point in setting them out here. There are many versions of Christianity in existence, and within Christianity there can be different viewpoints about almost everything.

Christian beliefs, values, practices and traditions are notable by their diversity – in fact, sometimes it's difficult to say 'Christians believe' (or 'do') without stereotyping and generalising to the point where the statement becomes meaningless. However, there are some fairly basic things which are likely to be believed by most Christians:

◆ There is a divine being, God, who exists and who cares for all things.

◆ This divine being sent his son, Jesus Christ as an example of how he wishes us to live.

◆ There is a spiritual dimension to life.

◆ There is a purpose for the Universe and therefore for all life in it.

Christians are aware that their faith has a complicated past, and that it can be – and has been – used as an excuse to do some less than pleasant things. However, they also argue that it has made great contributions to the development of the world and is something which can help you make sense of life. They believe that it is something of great value which will make your life, as well as the life of everything else, immeasurably richer if you follow its teachings.

Science in the 21st Century

We usually think of science as something that *is* rather than as something that we *do*. In fact it is both. There is a body of scientific knowledge which has a long history, but which is open to challenge and debate through scientific research and the evidence which results. There are many different branches of science, just as there are in Christianity, and the disagreements within the scientific community can be just as wide, varied and intense as they are within any religious system of belief. Some scientists will argue that science differs fundamentally from religion, in that it is not based on 'belief' or opinion but on the scientific method which is solidly based on evidence. Science tests out theories and hypotheses, and where the evidence repeatedly supports these they can be come elevated to the status of scientific laws. Science, too, is pretty much everywhere, from the word-processor upon which this book is being written to the mobile phone you probably have in your pocket. Although there is some diversity of approach in science (and often widely different opinions) science also has some basics which are accepted by all scientists:

◆ Science is based on a method which is strictly applied in all branches of science.

◆ This involves the methodical testing and re-testing of hypotheses through rigorous means.

◆ The conclusions reached are open to discussion from other scientists, which can mean results are supported or rejected.

◆ Science should be an objective activity where the conclusions reached are based on the evidence uncovered.

Scientists, too, know that science can be (and has been) used for good and evil. The science which has brought us vaccinations against deadly diseases has also brought us deadly weapons of mass destruction. However, scientists would argue that overall a scientific outlook on life is one which can equally make your life immeasurably richer.

Some Terminology

Throughout this book you will see some terminology (or labels) for the views you will come across. So here are some explanations:

Scientists/religious people: It is important to remember that many scientists are also religious people, and many religious people who are not scientists, accept the findings of science and may even accept some or all of the theories of science in relation to the topic areas of this course.

Scientists: Occasionally in this book the word 'scientist' will be used as a contrast to 'religious people' (but not always!).

Religious people: 'Religious people' will often be used as a contrast to 'science' or 'scientists'. Also remember that in this course, and therefore in this book, 'religious people' almost always refers to Christians.

Scientific materialists: This term is used in the SQA arrangements and refers specifically to people who understand the world in scientific (as opposed to religious) ways (such people may or may not be scientists!).

Religious Literalists: This refers to Christians who accept the teachings of Christianity (particularly those in the Bible) as literally, factually and historically true. The opposite of this group are those who interpret the Bible partly or wholly symbolically. You will sometimes find such people described as liberals.

Creationists: These are Christians who accept the Bible's teachings on the origins of the Universe and the origin and development of life on Earth as factually true accounts. They base their views on the Bible's teachings alone (though there are 'young Earth Creationists' and 'old Earth Creationists').

Creation Scientists: These are Christians who believe that God created the Universe and all life in it. However, they use scientific methods to support their views, not just the teachings of the Bible. This group are sometimes referred to as supporters of Intelligent Design.

Darwinists: These are people who support the evolutionary theories of Charles Darwin as set out in *The Origin of Species*.

'Neo-Darwinists' is the term given to those who accept a modified Darwinian theory based on findings which came after Darwin's lifetime.

Knowing Me, Knowing You

How do Christians and scientific materialists 'see' each other in the 21st Century? What is their relationship? This is a complex question, but it is important to get a feeling for the views of each category. This might help you understand where the 'heat' comes from in some of their arguments! There are all sorts of views here and they run on a spectrum from 'serious' to 'not serious' (or 'dangerous' to 'not dangerous' if you would like to think of it like that).

Christians on Scientific Materialists

At best, Christians think that scientific materialists are genuinely honest and caring people who are trying to make the world a better place through putting their science to good use. Their theories about the Universe and the life forms in it are open and honest attempts to make sense of the way things are, and in many cases they are right. They are simply humans searching for meaning, and they find it through scientific explanations. Their findings are independent from religious views because they apply in a different way to religion.

One view is that science is confused and confusing. Scientists are muddled about things and sometimes use their science to back up beliefs which they already hold.

They offer alternative explanations to religion, but these are unclear and unhelpful. They possibly spend too much time looking into things which aren't going to make life better for anyone. This leads to religion being questioned and challenged.

At worst, science is an arrogant process where scientists try to make themselves God by taking over 'roles' which only he should have (this applies to things like genetic engineering). This is an example of the 'fallen' human condition after the disobedience of Adam. Science is wide open to human misuse and has created things which humans aren't able to handle, things that appeal to our selfishness and inhumanity. Some scientists are directly anti-religious and do what they can to harm and challenge religious beliefs.

Scientific Materialists on Christians

At best, Christians are well-meaning people who use their beliefs, and the values that religion helps them develop, to make the world a better place. They are honestly searching for meaning in life and find it through religion, and many of their teachings are good ones. Their beliefs are completely independent of the scientific process.

In the middle of the spectrum is the view that Christians are mildly eccentric – people who believe in something which is really just a giant universal imaginary friend. This is usually (but not always) quite harmless. They spend too much time thinking about things which are ultimately just matters of 'you believe it or not'. Religion can have a tendency to dissuade people from trying to improve their own lives, instead accepting it all as 'God's will'.

At worst, religion is a dangerous superstition which has held human development back for too long. It has mostly given power to its priests, holy men and women, and been used to keep others in their place. It has been the excuse for many kinds of inhumanity throughout history, and replaces thinking with mindless obedience to a divine power. In some cases it is used to withhold the beneficial developments of science as they are seen to be 'playing God'.

Again, it is important to stress that some see science and Christianity as complete opposites and some do not. Hopefully you will be able to make up your own mind about that by the end of this book. It is hoped that you will learn about both religious and scientific ways of explaining things. It is also hoped, as with all the RMPS books by this author, that you don't do this simply for the sake of passing an exam (though I hope that you do), but that it forms part of your own exploration of what it means to be human and what your place in the Universe is all about (if anything). We all have our different views about what is right, wrong, true and false. Teachers even have different views about what should be studied and how it should be done. The aim of RMPS is to help you develop your understanding of these issues and also to reflect upon them and consider what they might mean in your life. Everything we learn and everything we examine in life should go into that pot of developing understanding – so that you can be truly human. The famous physicist Albert Einstein once said: 'Religion without science is lame; Science without religion is blind'.

Some Questions to Consider Before You Carry On

1 Do you think you understand 'life, the Universe and everything' in religious or scientific ways, or as a mixture of both?

2 What things in life do, or might, fill you with a sense of 'awe and wonder'?

3 What are your views on the existence of God?

4 Do you think science and religion are opposites?

5 In what ways do you think your life, community, country, society and world has been affected by religion?

6 In what ways do you think your life, community, country, society and world has been affected by science?

7 Are religion and science 'good' or 'bad' things?

8 Do you think humans are in any way 'special'? What might make us so?

9 What gives your life meaning?

Here's a wee conversation about revelation for your education...

Rab and Donnie are in Tieland ("A tie for every occasion"). It's not the kind of place you'd usually find them, but it is right next door to one of Rab's favourite places – Big Gordon's Pie Shop (which Big Gordon had originally called 'My Tie Pie' but changed it following too many phone calls asking for satay chicken and jasmine rice). Rab and Donnie are here because Donnie borrowed a film about Nicky Cruz from the video shop thinking it was an action film with Tom Cruise. Nevertheless, Donnie watched the film and was very taken with the story of how a violent gang member in New York could be turned from the dark side and now lives a good life as a Christian. So Donnie has begun to think that he might try Christianity, but Rab is beginning to wonder if Donnie has really got the hang of this faith yet, or in fact if Donnie will ever really get the hang of anything...

Rab: So you think you need a tie now that you're tryin' oot Christianity for size?

Donnie: It's all aboot presentin' myself tae the world in a new way Rab.

Rab: Well, which one are ye goin' for? Somethin' bright and zazzy or a wee bit merr muted? Mibbe merr beige...?

Donnie: Give me a wee mo here.

(While holding one tie in each hand, Donnie closes his eyes in a moment of what Rab thinks might be prayer. After a minute or so, during which Rab shuffles uncomfortably smiling at the other shoppers who have spotted Donnie's peculiar behaviour, Donnie chooses the yellow stripy tie.)

Rab: What, might I ask, wis aw that aboot?

Donnie: I wis asking God for some advice.

Rab: No, ye canny be serious… aboot which tie tae choose?

Donnie: Aye, why no? God reveals himsel' tae us aw the time, we just huv tae listen.

Rab: Do you actually think that the Big Man is up there havin' a wee natter wi' the angels aboot whether you should get the red spotty tie or the yellow stripy wan? You've hud some funny ideas over the years Donnie, but this wan really takes the biscuit.

Donnie: Ye see, there ye go again Rab, always the doubter. Can ye no just sometimes open your mind tae the possibilities?

Rab: Oh aye, I sometimes wonder if it's possible for you to be any merr unbelievably stupit.

Donnie: Look Rab, God doesny just boom a big voice oot the sky like in the movies. He speaks tae us in aw sorts of ways, showin' us what he wants for us, how he wants us tae live. He sends us examples like Moses and Jesus. He sometimes speaks right tae us – directly – wan tae wan.

Rab: Indeed Donnie, I've often wondered about how many voices are in your heid.

Donnie: Nae need to be a cynic Rab. He also speaks tae us through his holy word, the Bible.

Rab: Oh aye, of course, ah remember that bit well. Is it no in the book of Deuterogeronimo Chapter 666…"Thus spake the Lord: Thou shalt most definitely chooseth of the yellow stripy ties. Avoideth thee the red spotty wans, fur they are an abomination."

Donnie: Does it?

Rab: Aw Donnie… get real. Just fur a wee minute or two… it's fur yer own good.

Donnie: So ur ye telling me that aw these Christians who say God spoke tae them or guides them in their life ur just livin' in lalaland?

Rab: Naw, I'm no. Look I have nae doubt that Christians believe God guides them. Mibbe that is just through telling them stuff in the Bible. Mibbe it's through the examples of people who live the Christian life – and aye, it's might just be that he sneaks a wee helpful word right intae their brain every now and again. But let's get some perspective here Donnie. That'd be when he's tellin' them how tae live their lives, fight oppression, make big moral choices, choose their lifestyle, support their fellow humankind. It might even be when he's tellin' them why things ur the way they ur – how did it aw begin? How dae we find oot whit's true and whit's no – that kind of thing.

Not Donnie, most definitely not, which tie is the most likely wan tae choose tae express yur faith…

Donnie: Well, ah don't see why no. If God's intae aw your life then he can help ye choose yur tie as well can he no?

Rab: I'm sure he can Donnie, I just don't think he'd want tae. He might want tae let ye choose it all by yersel. Besides, I don't think Christians really believe that God reveals his nature tae ye through givin' ye fashion tips.

Donnie: Right, well mibbe I'll just choose a bow tie instead.

Rab: Naw Donnie, no a bow tie. Anythin' but a bow tie. Now that definitely wouldny go with yer army combat troosers, yer donkey jacket and yer checked shirt…

Talk Point ①

From what you know about Christianity so far, would God answer a prayer which asked him which tie you should wear?

Revelation in Christianity

Most Christians would probably chuckle at the idea of asking God which tie to wear. While Christians believe that God is involved in every aspect of their lives, they also think that there are some choices you just have to make for yourself. One of the important features of Christianity is that it is a **faith**. Your acceptance of it is based upon **belief** and is a matter of free choice. If God appeared to you and boomed out a command for you to follow him you would no longer be freely choosing to believe in him – because you would have the **proof** of his existence right there in your face. But Christians do believe that God has **revealed** his presence throughout the ages and continues to do so, although it's a bit more subtle than advising you on your dress sense. The way that he has revealed himself to humanity is, according to Christians, varied, but done in a way which makes sure you're not forced to believe in him.

Revelation of God's Nature

Christians believe that throughout history God has shown us who he is by what he does. In fact, the Hebrew name for God – which is never spoken out loud – is **YHWH** (Yahweh). This Hebrew word can only really be translated as "I AM", or – "I will show you who I am by what I do". So the very name of God is tied up with how he acts and what he does in various ways. For example, in giving the Commandments to Moses on Mount Sinai, God revealed to the Israelites the kind of life he wanted them to live. These instructions for living gave them some idea of the kind of God he was and continue to do so for Christians today. His nature was (and is) revealed through showing what matters to him.

Christians believe that throughout the period of what they call the Old Testament[1], he continued to **reveal** himself through guiding Kings, prophets and individuals in the way he wanted them to live – also showing that he was the kind of God who wanted to set up a relationship with his creation because he never seemed to give up, even when humanity rejected him.

For many Christians, the final and ultimate revelation of God was in the form of **Jesus**. Christians believe that Jesus was the **incarnation** of God – quite literally **God made flesh** – God in a human form come to Earth to experience life as one of his own creation and so show humans the way he wants them to live. In becoming human, God takes the initiative in revealing himself to humans. We don't have to go and find him, he came and found us.

[1]It is important to remember that Christians share a lot of biblical material with the Jewish faith. In fact, most of the "Christian" Bible is the Jewish scriptures (Tanakh). Jesus was, after all, Jewish – as were all of his first followers. In fact, some say he never intended to start a new religion, but to clarify Jewish teachings… but that's a whole other book… In this textbook, Christian scriptures refer to the Old and New Testaments.

Source 1

Revelation

By natural reason man can know God with certainty, on the basis of his works. But there is another order of knowledge, which man cannot possibly arrive at by his own powers: the order of divine Revelation. Through an utterly free decision, God has revealed himself and given himself to man. This he does by revealing the mystery, his plan of loving goodness, formed from all eternity in Christ, for the benefit of all men. God has fully revealed this plan by sending us his beloved Son, our Lord Jesus Christ, and the Holy Spirit.

Comment: God makes himself known to his creation – humanity – through the person of Jesus. Jesus therefore acts as a role model of the kind of person God would want us to be.

Catechism of the Roman Catholic Church at http://www.vatican.va/archive/catechism/p1s1c2a1.htm

Talk Point   2

Looking at the natural world... what might it say about the kind of being people might believe God to be?

Revelation of God through Scripture

For many Christians, the scriptures of the **Bible** are the main way in which God has revealed himself to humanity. This holy book has been passed down throughout the ages to become what we have today and in its contents you can find what God wants for his creation. Of course, as you might have guessed, it's not just as simple as that and different Christians have different views about what scripture can tell us about God and his plans for humanity. Here are just some of the varied viewpoints within Christianity:

◆ The Bible is **divinely inspired**: This could mean that the writers of the Bible were guided by God when they were writing the Bible down. Some see this as a kind of 'possession' – where the Holy Spirit takes the writer over and writes through him (or her, but that's a whole other issue!) This would mean that every word of the Bible is actually the word of God himself, channelled through a human writer.

◆ The Bible is **divinely guided**: This is the same as the above without the element of supernatural possession. God simply speaks to the writers in some way or other, who then write what they think God wants them to – it's a little less dramatic but amounts to the same thing and means that the Bible is still the direct word of God.

◆ The Bible is the end result of a lot of God's mysterious guidance throughout the ages. The Bible is in fact a library of stories and writings from different time periods, cultures and geographical locations. Some of the writing is history; poetry, letters and stories and so on. This has all been passed down through the ages, sometimes just by word of mouth. Eventually it was selected by humans to become part of what we now have as the Bible. However, throughout this long and complex process, God was closely involved – making sure that his plans and teachings were clearly 'in' the Bible. This, of course, still means that the Bible is the word of God, but that you have to separate out what is there into what might be God's word and what might be something which was written in a particular time for a specific reason.

◆ The Bible is a **human book**, but based on the writings of people who have tried to work out what God would want throughout the ages. What is in the Bible is a matter of human selection and the different forms of writing are to be understood in different ways – however, it is still essentially a useful book of guidance for someone trying to live a Christian life, as it contains things which have been judged helpful in allowing us to understand what the faith is all about.

There are probably many more understandings of what the Bible represents, but for this course, there are really three ways we will treat Bible writings in this book:

◆ **Literally** true: What the Bible says is what happened – exactly, word for word – no argument about it. People who believe this are sometimes called **Biblical literalists** (or Christian literalists).

◆ **Symbolically** true: Biblical writings have to be understood as pointing to truths – metaphors and allegories and so on, but not to be taken as literally true. People who believe this are sometimes called **Biblical liberals** (or Liberal Christians).

◆ **Part literal, part symbolic**: Biblical writings are a mixture of things which are literally true and things which need to be interpreted. Which is which would be a matter of debate…

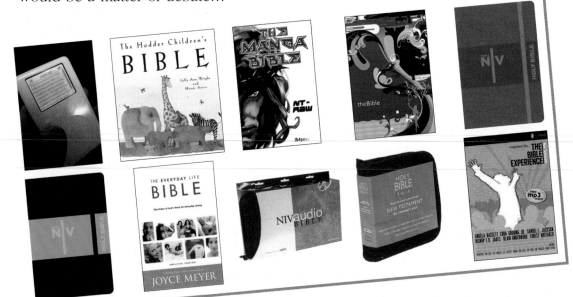

Sources 2 and 3

Bible Truth 1

The hierarchy of the Roman Catholic Church has published a teaching document instructing the faithful that some parts of the Bible are not actually true.

The Catholic bishops of England, Wales and Scotland are warning their five million worshippers, as well as any others drawn to the study of scripture, that they should not expect "total accuracy" from the Bible.

"We should not expect to find in Scripture full scientific accuracy or complete historical precision," they say in *The Gift of Scripture*.

Comment: This article goes on to describe the kinds of things which are considered to be true in the Bible and those which are not. The Catholic Bishops make a distinction between 'religious' matters in the Bible which are true and 'secular' matters which we should not expect to be written about with 'total accuracy'.

Bible Truth 2

What God recorded in Genesis is absolutely perfect! But it is not all that God wants us to know about Him. Only the full collection of 66 inspired books is both perfect and complete.

Comment: This source comes from a website called Whitcomb Ministries and is by Professor John D Whitcomb. This quote is from a talk he gave in 1995 celebrating the 25th anniversary of the founding of the Institute for Creation research (which you will find out more about later). This organisation supports the Bible teaching that God made the Universe in 6 days – exactly as the Bible teaches. It believes that the Bible is literally true in every respect.

http://www.timesonline.co.uk/tol/news/world/europe/article574768.ece

*http://www.whitcombministries.org/Biblical_Articles/
The_Significance_Of_Genesis_1-11.php*

One problem of course is that the Bible is sometimes quite complex. Understanding it properly might mean that you have to know something about:

◆ The history of the places in which it was written.

◆ What their culture was like, what things mattered to them, their laws and values and so on.

◆ Their language and uses of language.

It sounds like you need a PhD to understand the Bible – and some argue that because it is such a complex book, we need to be very careful about making claims that it definitely says one thing or another. **Interpretation** of the Bible (or close reading) is an area of study in its own right, and not simple. So when someone states that: 'the Bible says…' perhaps we should be asking, 'when, to whom and why…?' However, some Christians argue that even though the Bible is quite complex, God provides ways to help us understand what it contains.

Talk Point

3

Do people read the Bible these days?

Strengths and Limitations of this Kind of Revelation

Strengths	Limitations
• The Bible is quite clear and can be read by anyone so it's obvious what its messages are.	• The Bible may appear clear but it is a complicated text. Although it can be read by anyone, not everyone understands the language or the world in which it was written and so may not be a good guide for modern living.
• This means that we have God's direct word on what he is like and how we should live our lives.	• It may be God's word, but it might also involve human hands which have written things or selected things for inclusion which are there for human purposes, not divine ones.

Strengths	Limitations
• This means you don't have to guess about anything – everything which is important to know can be understood by reading the Bible and so it is a reliable way to find out about God and what he wants for humans.	• You may not need to 'guess', but interpreting the Bible is a complex task and so it might not be a very reliable way to find out about God or about his wants and desires.
• If you understand the Bible literally then it is simple to work out the truth of what God is and what he wants.	• If you do not understand the Bible literally then you need to work out what is truth and what is myth and so on.

General and Special Revelation

As well as believing in revelation through scripture, Christians believe that God reveals himself to his creation in many different ways. These can be grouped as **general** and **special** revelations.

General Revelation

This is where God reveals his character and therefore his wants and desires through what he does. This can be seen through his acts of creation. Many Christians point to the order and complexity of the natural world and say that it points to an all-powerful creator which they call God – more of that later. They also say that throughout human history, God has revealed himself through his actions, in delivering humans from suffering or acting in other ways to show who he is. Also, general revelation can mean simply an awareness that God is around through what he does in the individual. Some say that the human conscience is actually God's voice, quietly and gently reminding us of who we are as well as what we can be.

Sources 4 and 5

Bible Revelations

The heavens declare the glory of God: The skies proclaim the work of his hands.

For since the beginning of the world God's invisible qualities – his eternal power and the divine nature – have been clearly seen, being understood from what has been made, so that men are without excuse.

Comment: The first Bible text makes it quite clear – look around you, what you see points to God. Paul's letter to the Romans supports this idea and suggests that it would be hard to deny God's existence having looked around you at the creation.

Psalm 19:1
Romans 1:20

God's work?

Special Revelation

Throughout history, God has chosen to reveal himself to humans in much more direct or special ways, for example, through:

◆ Specific miracles – such as the parting of the red sea or the feeding of the five thousand.

◆ Visions – such as the vision of Saul on the road to Damascus.

◆ Dreams – such as those of Joseph.

◆ 'Appearances' – such as the burning bush or the delivery of the commandants on Mount Sinai.

◆ Speaking directly – such as when he spoke to Samuel.

◆ Finally, Christians believe that God revealed his nature to them by **becoming human** in the form of **Jesus**. Jesus was an example both of how to live a human life, but also a glimpse of the nature of God – and you don't get a lot more special than that.

Talk Point

4

What would you do if you thought that God had spoken to you in a dream?

Sources 6 and 7

Revelation through Jesus

"Through the incarnation God descended into nature in order to super-animate and take it back to him."

"Thanks to the multitude of individuals and vocations, the Spirit of God insinuates itself everywhere and is everywhere at work."

Comment: Pierre Teilhard de Chardin (1881–1951) was a Jesuit Priest. He believed that God revealed himself to humans through Jesus who was God's supreme way of making himself known to us, and through his spirit in the world. He argued that humans would not find meaning in material things but only in spiritual ones.

*Pierre Teilhard de Chardin: Mysticism of Science, 1939, VI, 178 quoted at
http://www.teilharddechardin.org/teilharddechardin.pdf*

*Pierre Teilhard de Chardin: The Divine Milieu, page 93 quoted at
http://www.catholic-library.org.uk/quotes-of-note.html*

Strengths and Limitations of this Kind of Revelation

Strengths	Limitations
• If we look at nature we can infer (work out) the existence of an all-powerful God and get some idea of the power of such a being	• Nature could just as well point to other creative processes – none of which need a God (such as evolution)
• Nature points to God's power	• Nature might just as equally point to a God who has created a pretty violent form of existence for most living creatures
• A conscience might point to the existence of a supernatural being	• A conscience could just as well be the workings of the human brain
• Miracles and supernatural happenings all point to a God who has power over the laws of physics	• Miracles and supernatural happenings are just exaggerated stories or things which were misunderstood at the time – mind over matter as opposed to the existence of a God
• The voice of God can have no other explanation than the existence of a God	• People hear voices in their head and do some very strange things – it certainly doesn't automatically point to the existence of a God
• Jesus was God in human form and so the ultimate revelation of who God is and how he thinks we should live	• Jesus was just a good man – maybe even one who thought he was a God, but there's no solid proof that Jesus was God
• God's appearances throughout human history show his desire to reveal himself to us	• God's appearances seem to have become a little less dramatic in recent times

Some people argue that God seemed to be a lot more present in the past than he is today because he revealed himself much more directly then compared to now. Others argue that God still reveals himself today – we just don't listen so well nowadays… What do you think?

Revelation through the Traditions of the Church

Christians also believe that God has revealed himself throughout the ages through the traditions of **the Church**. For this we need a whirlwind ecclesiastical history lesson, very much simplified:

After Jesus died, the disciples hid away and then came out three days later to proclaim that he had risen from the dead. They formed a small Jewish sect in a Roman World and had a hard time of it through persecution. Each disciple, it is said, took the new faith to different lands. The apostle Paul finally spread it to the non-Jewish (Gentile) world, explaining very Jewish ideas in ways that non-Jews could understand. The persecutions continued until the Roman Emperor Constantine made Christianity the official religion of the Empire. One Christian Church now existed, but the leaders of the church in important cities across the known world each thought they were the true church. Eventually, two cities held the real power of the Christian Church – Rome and Constantinople. However, the church remained one organisation until there was a split in 1054 between the East – Constantinople and the West – Rome. It was now split into two – the Roman Catholic Church and the Orthodox Church. Both had their own internal disputes, but a major split came to the West in the 16th Century when Martin Luther broke away from the Church and so began the split between Protestants and Catholics in the West. The Protestant Church itself split into many different groups as it is today – Baptists, Quakers, Methodists and so on…

Throughout all of this, each church developed its own traditions and ways of doing things as well as focussing on different aspects of belief. Each church group believed that it was doing what God wanted and so its **traditions** – both beliefs and practices, revealed the kind of being God was (and is). You should be aware that for most of the history of Christianity, ordinary people were often not able to read and so depended on the leaders of the churches to explain the

faith to them and give them guidance about their religious life. Even today, when people are able to read scriptures and understand them for themselves, they are often so complex and so linked to history that understanding them is helped by turning to important teachers in the church to help ordinary believers make sense of them. This still means that each Church holds some kind of power over what is 'the truth', and it is sometimes so complicated that ordinary people can only follow the Church's traditions in faith and trust.

One problem with this is that the traditions of the churches are sometimes so linked to time, place and culture that it makes it difficult to know what might be revelation from God and what might just be habit. However, many Christians believe that church **leaders** are chosen – or called – by God to these roles, therefore what they say is, in some way, approved of by God.

Example 1: In the Roman Catholic Church there are no women priests. This is Church tradition and reflects the belief that God made men and women to carry out different roles in life, and also reflects the fact that Jesus did not choose any female disciples. This is much more complex than we can go into here, but it's an example of how the Church's tradition reflects a particular belief about God's wishes. However, other branches of the Christian church have women priests – which church has got it right? Which one is God revealing himself to us through?

Example 2: Some Christian churches baptise babies to welcome them into the church. Others have believers' baptism – where only adults who understand what they are doing are baptised. Again, the tradition of infant or believer's baptism says something about what these Churches believe the nature of God – and people's relationship to him – is. However, other churches do not have baptisms at all – which church is right? Which one is God revealing himself to us through?

Strengths and Limitations of this Kind of Revelation

Strengths	Limitations
• The Church has maintained its traditions for two thousand years. This is a pretty firm foundation upon which to base our belief in God.	• The Church has changed so much over a mere two thousand years that it cannot be a very reliable messenger of what God is and what he wants. Some of its 'old' beliefs would be considered very unacceptable in today's world.
• The Church is full of people whom God has called to represent him, and so reveals who he is and what he wants.	• The Church is an organisation of humans and as such has all the problems associated with that. Its teachings are far too mixed up with culture, politics and history to tell us anything all that meaningful about the nature of God.
• The Church's leadership has provided a stable foundation for people's beliefs throughout its history.	• The leadership of the Church has been anything but stable and certainly not something which can reveal God to us.

Talk Point

6

Do you think that the Christian church is as central in the world today as it once was? Is this something we should be concerned about?

Simple Section Summary

◆ Christianity is a faith.
◆ This faith is based on the belief that God has revealed himself to us.
◆ God has revealed his nature by his actions throughout history.
◆ His final revelation for Christians comes in the form of Jesus.
◆ So Jesus shows us what God is really like.
◆ God also reveals himself through the Bible.
◆ Some Christians think the Bible is the literal word of God.
◆ Some think that the Bible's writing were 'guided' by God.
◆ Some think the Bible is just a human book.
◆ The Bible might be literally true, symbolically true or a mixture of both.
◆ God may speak directly to people or show himself through his actions.
◆ The natural world may reveal the character of God.
◆ The Church sees itself as God's representative on Earth.
◆ The beliefs and actions of the Church may therefore give us an idea of what God is like.

Revelation through Religious Experience

Because of many of the problems associated with interpreting Scripture and following the example of the church, many Christians throughout the ages have argued that the only reliable way for God to reveal himself to us is through a **direct experience** of him communicating with us. **Religious experience** can come in lots of different ways:

◆ An experience of completeness or 'one-ness'. This can be a momentary flash where everything seems to work itself out. It can be a slow-dawning realisation that things maybe aren't what they seem. Some people think of this as 'becoming one' with the Universe or sensing the presence of God. This is sometimes called having an experience of **the numinous**.

◆ A reaction to some event. People look for meaning in all sorts of things and for some, the more powerful the experience the greater the possible 'meaning' behind it (though often religious experiences happen over what you might think are pretty ordinary happenings). For example, someone who survives a serious illness – especially when they weren't expected to survive – will often understand this as having a meaning. They might think it is telling them to look at their own life and live it for a different reason. Some people feel called by God to do all sorts of things – change their lives, work with the poor, become a missionary and so on. These callings may be accompanied by a 'feeling' of being called by God – a religious experience.

Religious experiences can be very dramatic – people report seeing angels, Mary, Jesus – or God himself. They may see visions, have dreams or be visited by deceased relatives. They may happen during worship or following some 'miraculous' event. However, they can also be less dramatic – just a simple awareness of having received some kind of direct communication from God.

Source 8

Religious Experience

Now, it is theoretically possible that [religious experiences are] delusory. It is also no less possible that through [religious experiences] we are being affected by the reality and presence of a transcendent creative power... releasing new possibilities within us... my claim is that in this situation it is entirely reasonable, rational, appropriate and sane for us to... positive response, the response of faith...

Comment: This book is a debate between John Hick, a Christian and Michael Goulder, a former Christian Priest who no longer believes in God. Goulder's response to Hick's claim that religious experience is reasonable evidence of God's revelation concludes with, among others, the following points:

◆ We think it's irrational to trust experiences for which there's no evidence. Such evidence is lacking in experiences of God.

◆ Hick seems to argue that religious experiences can have psychological explanations and that sometimes these are all that religious experiences are. He doesn't explain how anyone might be able to tell the difference.

◆ Hick doesn't explain why many religious people who seek to find the presence of God do not have religious experiences while people not seeking them sometimes do. This seems unfair.

John Hick in 'Why Believe in God?' Page 47

*Comment points based on pages 62–63 of Goulder, M & Hick, J;
Why Believe in God? SCM Press (1983)*

In *The Varieties of Religious Experience* (1902), William James described the main stages of a typical religious experience (though religious experiences can be very varied):

◆ the experience is short and quite intense
◆ you have no control over it
◆ it helps you see things in a different way
◆ it is very difficult to describe – only others who have had such experiences have even the slightest hope of understanding what you've gone through.

Someone having a 'Religious Experience' is much more common than you probably think, and the experiences are similar enough to make us wonder if they are pointing to a God who chooses to reveal himself to us in this way. The fact that such experiences almost always change people's lives for the better – and really quite drastically – perhaps suggests that they could only come from God…

Talk Point

7

Why do some people seem to have religious experiences and others do not?

Strengths and Limitations of this Kind of Revelation

Strengths	Limitations
• These experiences are almost always life-changing – they often happen to people whose lives are troubled and after them they change their whole way of life for the better. In fact, many of the world's great religions were started by individuals who had what we would call a religious experience (e.g. Buddha's enlightenment, Muhammad's experience in receiving the Qur'an).	• People's lives change for all sorts of reasons – using their strange experiences to prove the existence of a God isn't all that reliable a way to do so.

Strengths	Limitations
• The people who have them feel that they are very real – they point to a spiritual dimension to life. This means that they can't be proved in any scientific way because the spiritual dimension is beyond the reach of scientific investigation.	• 'Religious Experiences' can lead to negative consequences too. People who have them may end up doing bad things and not good ones. Cult leaders often end up committing terrible acts following 'religious experiences'. Also, history is full of people who did bad things because 'voices in their head' told them to.
• People don't make them happen – they just happen – sometimes quite unexpectedly and to the least likely people. This strengthens the possibility that they are real.	• More people do not have them than do. Why would God let some people have religious experiences and not others? Why would some people be 'saved' from dangerous situations and others not? Why would some be given this help to change their lives and others not?
• They have happened throughout history and all over the world and often they are very similar. Surely so many people can't be kidding themselves?	• Perhaps religious experiences only 'happen' to people who are suggestible – or to people who have altered brain chemistry. This could happen through emotion, illness, drugs – or just the frenzy of a religious ceremony
• If they happen in some kind of 'spiritual dimension' then there's not much we can say about them. Why would God choose to reveal himself in a way which is so open to doubt?	• Religious experiences have happened throughout history and all over the world – but something happening to a million people doesn't automatically make it more reliable.

People who believe in religious experiences as proof of the revelation of God argue that because they are so **personal** and so **unique** they could only come from God. Those who think religious experiences are not things which have come from a God say that they are so unique and so personal that it's meaningless to talk about them unless you've had one. Surely a God would not reveal himself in this strange way when he could do so in a much more obvious and less disputable way?

Revelation through Order and Design

Many religious people argue that you don't need supernatural events to show that God reveals himself to us – all you have to do is look around you. The Universe seems **just right** (this is sometimes called the **Goldilocks Effect**, after the fairy story) for the existence and survival of life (well on Earth it does anyway) – this points to a creator. **Nature** reveals God to us – in that it shows us who he is and the kind of being he is – as well as the kind of beings we should be. **Design** comes in two forms:

◆ Design qua **purpose** – everything in the Universe seems just right for the 'job' it has to do – this points to some divine hand at work behind it all.

◆ Design qua **regularity** – the Universe is full of order when it could just as well be a chaotic mess. This order again points to the existence of a God.

We'll come back to this in more detail when looking at Areas 2 and 3, but for the moment all you need to be clear about is this: according to Christians, God reveals himself through the **structure and order of the natural world**. Only an all-powerful being could be behind the creation and maintenance of the Universe. The order, beauty and regularity of the Universe is God's way of communicating his existence to us and telling us something about the kind of being he is.

Talk Point 8

Does the existence of the Universe point to the existence of a creator?

Strengths and Limitations of this Kind of Revelation

Strengths	Limitations
• You cannot deny the existence of the Universe or its vastness and incredible complexity. Such a thing could not have come about by chance and therefore points to the existence of a creator.	• The Universe is vast and complex but why does that need to point to any creator? In fact, you just double your problem, because if there's an even more vast and complex creator then it begs the obvious question – where did his creator come from? It's just as likely that the Universe has no creator as it is that God has no creator.
• Nature's beauty and order point to a loving God who cares about his creation – enough to maintain the perfect conditions for the existence of life.	• Nature may appear beautiful but it is full of violence and suffering – in fact the only way that living things survive is by taking advantage of the death of other things in one way or another – doesn't point to a very loving creator at all…

Why is Revelation Important in Christianity?

Christians believe God reveals himself in many different ways. Some of these are open to scientific enquiry and some are not. Some refer to '**spiritual**' events and some to **historical** ones. All can be the subject of debate and argument – and they are, as you shall soon see. Christians believe that God has tried to communicate with his creation right from the beginning and has tried many different ways of doing so. According to Christians, some listen and understand and some don't.

However the question is, why does it matter? Surely it's more important just to get on with our lives and let God do what he does – but not according to Christians. Christians argue that we can only really understand ourselves and our purpose in life when we recognise and accept the existence of God. This recognition and acceptance will affect us not just in this life but for all eternity. It is tied up with the very question of who we are, where we came from and where we are going. So, the revelation of God is crucial to our existence – or rather, us recognising and responding to God's revelation is crucial. According to Christianity, God reveals himself to us in many different ways – and it is important for us to listen.

Simple Section Summary

◆ Religious experience is believed to be direct experience of God.
◆ It can come in many different forms.
◆ The experience reveals the nature of God.
◆ Religious experiences are very personal and unique.
◆ So they may be unique revelations about God – valuable for everyone.
◆ Or they might be meaningful only for the person who has them.
◆ God may reveal himself through order in nature.
◆ The structure and design of the Universe might point to the character of God.
◆ Understanding God's revelation is central to the life of a Christian.
◆ It helps give meaning to all aspects of life.

The Strengths and Limitations of Revelation Summarised

Strengths	Limitations
• God chooses to reveal his nature and existence to the things he has created. He doesn't need to but chooses to. This suggests that we are important to him and there is a reason for his revelation.	• All of the ways in which God has 'revealed' himself to us are ambiguous – they're all open to debate, argument and disagreement. They could all be interpreted in different ways, and because they are so debatable they're not very reliable.

Strengths	Limitations
• He has revealed himself throughout history and continues to do so in many different ways, such as through scripture, visions, religious experience, miracles, the traditions of the church and the order and design found in nature.	• Humans find things out through investigating, testing and using evidence. The 'evidence' for God which comes from the kinds of revelation examined so far is not very strong. If God wanted to reveal himself to us, why not just do it in a more obvious way which would definitely not be open to debate. The forms of revelation we have looked at so far just don't work and don't really explain who God is or what he wants.
• Christians believe that the person of Jesus – God made flesh – is the ultimate revelation of who God is and how he wants us to live	• It is not clear how far the 'Jesus story' is 'as it happened' or 'as it was later edited by the Church'.

Activities

Knowledge, Understanding, Analysis and Evaluation

1 Why was Rab surprised at Donnie's praying in the tie shop?

2 According to Donnie, in what ways has God revealed himself?

3 Why might God avoid making a personal appearance to Donnie?

4 Explain why Christians think of Jesus as the 'ultimate revelation of God'.

5 Some people think that the Bible is 'divinely inspired'. What does this mean?

6 What does it mean when someone says that the Bible is 'literally true'?

7 What are the advantages and disadvantages for Christians who believe that the Bible is literally true?

8 What is the difference between interpreting the Bible literally and in a liberal way?

9 What factors might you need to have some understanding of before you can understand Bible writings?

10 State one strength and one limitation of using scripture as a way of understanding God's revelation.

11 Explain the difference between general and special revelation.

12 Describe in detail, with an example, one form of special revelation.

13 Describe one strength of special revelation.

14 What is meant by the 'tradition of the church'?

15 Give one reason why a Christian might follow the teachings of a Church leader.

16 Explain why someone might argue that the example of the Church is not a very good way to find God.

17 Describe one form of religious experience.

18 Explain one problem associated with religious experience.

19 According to William James, what are the key features of a religious experience?

20 Do you think religious experience is proof that there is a God? Give reasons for your answer.

21 Explain the difference between design qua purpose and design qua regularity.

22 Is the existence of the Universe enough proof that there is a God? Explain your answer.

23 In your own words, explain why God's revelation is important for Christians.

Active Learning

1 Find out what the Ten Commandments are. What do these suggest about the nature of God?

2 As a class, illustrate each of the Ten Commandments in artwork.

3 Make a list of things you think are acceptable to pray for and things which are not. If possible, give this list to a Christian and see what s/he thinks of it.

4 In the Old Testament, God's name was given as YHWH. When Jewish people read this in scriptures they say 'Shem' or 'Adonoi'. Find out why.

5 God did make 'personal appearances' in the Old Testament such as at the burning bush, on Mount Sinai and to Samuel. Find out what happened on these occasions and discuss what they might tell us about the nature of God.

6 If Jesus tells us about God's nature, what is he telling us?

7 What is the Holy Spirit? What is the relationship between the Holy Spirit, God and Jesus?

8 The Bible is full of different kinds of writing. Find out what these are. Does this make the Bible clearer or less clear as a way of finding out who God is and what he wants?

9 Some people believe that because the Christian Church is always changing, it is not a very reliable way to find God. Find out about some examples of change in the Christian Church. What things has the Church changed its views about over the years? What variety of beliefs is present within Christianity today?

10 Using the website in the Homework task below, find some examples of religious experience. What are the common features? What other explanations might be given for them?

11 Find out about someone who had a religious experience which changed their life. Create a class display on this person and the change which they experienced.

12 Create a class display: 'Order in Nature/Disorder in Nature'.

Unit Assessment Question

Higher:
According to Christians, how might God reveal himself? **KU8**

Intermediate 2:
What might a Christian mean by saying that 'God reveals himself through nature'? **KU0 AE4**

Sample Exam Question

Higher:
Explain one way in which the idea of revelation in the Christian tradition might be limited. **AE6**

Intermediate 2:
'Reading the Bible is the best way to find out about God.' Do you agree? Give two reasons for your answer. **AE4**

Homework

Find out about the work of the Alistair Hardy Research Centre into religious experience at http://www.lamp.ac.uk/aht/
Make a short report of your findings to present to your class.
Is religious experience evidence of God's revelation?

Personal Reflection

Should people let their lives be guided by Holy Scriptures? What might be helpful and unhelpful about living your life this way? Should Christians expect God to direct every single choice in their life?

Once upon a time there was a little girl who, very strangely, went by the name of 'Little red riding hood'. Thankfully her friends shortened this, equally strangely, to Agnes. Every week young Agnes would get dressed up in her red riding cape – though she never rode – and visit her Granny deep in the woods. She'd take Granny some sweeties and flowers in a little wicker basket. Granny always looked forward to Agnes's visits because she didn't get out much, and Agnes could keep Granny up to date with all the interesting gossip from the outside world. So, one fine day, having walked through the woods – always on the lookout for the fierce creatures which might snatch and eat an unsuspecting young traveller – Agnes arrived at the door of Granny's house.

"Knockitty knockitty knock knock knock!" shouted Agnes at the door – which was a funny little habit she'd recently developed, much to Granny's confusion. "Just use the bell dear" she'd say. However, it did the trick as the door soon opened. "Well" said Agnes, "We really must get you some of that mouthwash stuff Granny – your breath smells like you've just eaten a round of blue cheese followed by garlic ice cream!" Fortunately Granny was a little hard of hearing so she often missed some of Agnes's more acid comments – though today, Agnes had the funny feeling that Granny had heard every word.

"Oh, do come in little... eh... girl. How lovely to see you"

"It's Agnes Granny – your memory playing up again?"

"Pardon?" said Granny. "I didn't quite catch that... Agnes"

➡

"Mmm" thought Agnes – "something's a bit fishy here and it's not just Granny's mouth hygiene..."

"Come on, warm yourself by the fire dear. I'll just put the kettle on and make us a nice cup of tea" said Granny in the sweetest tones – though a little more gruffly than usual.

"Kettle?" Agnes began to think that something wasn't quite right. Granny only ever drank a decaf latte with skimmed milk... and what about Granny's slightly hairier-than-usual face. Now Agnes knew that Granny was growing a bit of a beard, but she'd always looked after herself in that respect... Agnes took off her red riding hood and laid it carefully on the chair. She had a hunch that she might be in need of some freedom of movement soon...

"Granny, were you up late watching Big Brother live again last night? Your eyes look awfully big today."

"Oh, all the better to see you with my dear."

"And Granny", Agnes continued a little more quietly, "What big ears you have. I've never... really... noticed them before."

"All the better to hear you with, sweetheart."

"And... goodness gracious me," Agnes added, in barely a whisper, "what big teeth you have."

"Yes my little one... all the better to eat you with!" at which Granny threw off her Granny clothes, got down onto all four paws and prepared to strike.

"Hah, I thought so!" yelled Agnes. "You're a great big foul-smelling bloodthirsty wolf!"

"Indeed I am, and a hungry one – there wasn't much meat on your Granny, but you'll do nicely for pudding I think!"

"Well... actually... nae chance. You see, you might have taken a little time to find out about me from Granny, or even tried out a few clever questions for yourself. Granny might have mentioned that I'm Scottish junior Taekwondo champion and a black belt of the 21st Dan. That makes me... unbeatable – and it makes you... dead meat!"

At this, Agnes swung round in a barely perceptible movement and, with the palm of her hand – in what looked to the untrained eye like nothing more than a gentle stroke– separated the wolf's head from his body.

"Wolves really ought to do their homework" said Agnes, as she checked to make sure she hadn't broken a fingernail...

We All Do Science

Agnes may have been a dab hand at the martial arts, but she was also a very sharp **scientist**. She started with a basic hunch – a gut feeling if you like – and moved from that to a fairly reasonable conclusion that Granny was more wolf than sweet little old lady. It's just as well Agnes was such a good scientist because it would have been a rather unfortunate mistake otherwise. (Imagine the conversation: "Well Detective Chief Inspector, I had this funny idea that the headless dead body now on the floor beside you was actually a walking, talking wolf dressed up as my Granny… ha ha… how wrong can you be eh?")

What Agnes did – remarkably quickly – is called **scientific method**. We all do it every day, and sometimes concerning the most everyday and not-at-all scientific things. So, what did Agnes actually do?

- ◆ **Observed** and pulled together her information (**data**): She noticed that some of Granny's typical behaviours and typical physical features didn't seem quite right.

- ◆ **Discarded possibilities** that didn't seem to work as **alternative explanations**: Granny's beard might have grown but it couldn't possibly have grown that thick in just a week.

- ◆ Came up with a guess, or **hypothesis**, that the creature before her wasn't granny but some hairy, foul-smelling, pointy-eared, sharp-toothed being (the features in question were pretty wolf-like).

- ◆ Tested out her **hypothesis** by doing some **research** into 'Granny's' behaviour and appearance (in this case a semi-structured, non-clinical interview).

- ◆ **Verified** her hypothesis (this would obviously be a one-tailed hypothesis) that 'Granny might be a wolf' by provoking decidedly wolf-like behaviour.

- ◆ Once her theory was **verified**, she **generalised** and **predicted** that other things should now **follow** (in this case, that hungry wolves are likely to eat little girls and so she'd better take some action to avoid that possibility).

This could all lead to a new scientific **law** or **theory** which others could draw upon in similar situations (in this case that Grannies who are ridiculously hairy, foul-smelling, with pointy ears and fangs are likely to fall into the scientific classification of vicious little-girl-eating-wolves – or maybe a new category of Granny of course).

Additionally, if Agnes's questions hadn't proved conclusive she could have carried out a small **experiment**

(she actually did so by speaking ever more quietly to test out 'Granny's' unusually good hearing that day'). Alternatively she could have done as follows: Agnes knows that Granny hates tea – in fact, it makes her physically sick. She could have allowed the wolf/Granny to make some tea and then observed the creature drinking it. If the creature had shown the slightest bit of enjoyment while drinking the tea then Agnes would have further verified her hypothesis that what stood before her was not Granny, and taken appropriate action based on a likely prediction about wolf behaviour. Furthermore, Agnes might have written up her method as peer-referenced scientific paper such as:

An inductive reasoning approach to establishing the identity of potentially murderous wolves masquerading as your Granny: Hood, L.R.R. Journal of Scientific Ridiculousness 2009 Vol X pp 142–235.

This paper would allow others to **replicate** what Agnes did in a similar situation and so support or reject Agnes's research findings. So, what Agnes did was something we all do – every day. Suppose you leave your class to go to the toilet. On your return, you observe that the people sitting around you are smirking and giggling to themselves. Your RMPS teacher tells them to get over themselves and stop being so nasty. You might think that their smirking and giggling was somehow at your expense, and you would probably investigate further using the method above to verify your hypothesis that there's something going on and it has something to do with you…

Talk Point 9

Using the scientific method above, discuss what you might do to find out what's going on. What hypotheses might you come up with? How might you test them? What would count as evidence?

Source 9

Scientific Method

It seems that we are forced to concede that conclusions arrived at inductively are never absolutely secure in the logical manner of deductive conclusions, even though 'common sense' is based on induction. That inductive reasoning is so often successful is a (remarkable) property the world that one might characterise as the 'dependability of nature'… In practice… human intellectual endeavour does not always proceed through deductive and inductive reasoning. The key to major scientific advances often rests with free-ranging imaginative leaps or inspiration.

Comment: Davies argues that inductive reasoning is open to interpretation. He cites the argument that just because the Sun rises every day and has always done so is not a 100% guarantee that it will always do so in future. However, science does build such 'imaginative leaps' into scientific method, though such leaps should always be subject to the rigours of scientific testing.

Paul Davies: The Mind of God: Science and the Search for Ultimate Meaning pp27–28

Scientific Method Further Explained

The particular version of scientific method you have looked at so far is called the **inductive method**. Here, we go from general **observations** to specific **theories** then scientific **laws** through a process of testing, retesting and verifying our **hypotheses.** If the evidence that we gather fits our hypothesis then our hypothesis is **supported** (NEVER proved). If the evidence seems to go against our hypothesis then we might try refining the tests we are using if we're still convinced that our hypothesis is true to see if that makes any difference – but there will come a point where we will have to abandon or **reject** our hypothesis because the evidence does not support it.

This means that 'scientific facts' are always open to the possibility that new evidence will bring them into question – or perhaps even new ways of understanding the old evidence. That's what science is in fact, it is a process rather than a destination, a method rather than just a set of facts to be learned. Scientific theory is always open to challenge and modification and for scientists that's one of its good points. It is not about belief or about holding onto things even when they don't seem right, it's about listening to the evidence and changing your theories to fit the evidence – never the other way around.

Strengths and Limitations of Inductive Scientific Reasoning

Strengths	Limitations
• The method is an effective way to follow up observations with systematic testing.	• We have to begin by observing, and sometimes we might not 'see' anything worth testing and even if we do it's still open to interpretation.
• It takes into account alternative possibilities and puts these to the test.	• We would need to be sure that all the alternative possibilities had been considered.
• It produces testable hypotheses.	• Hypotheses reached may still be based on our interpretation of what we observe and so may be an inaccurate or misleading starting-point for our research.

Strengths	Limitations
• It can be verified or falsified.	• What counts as 'verified' or 'falsified' is still subject to our interpretation of the evidence.
• It leads to laws and theories, which cover all similar instances.	• Laws and theories derived during this method may still not cover every apparently similar instance.
• The method can be replicated by others and so our findings supported or rejected.	• *Exact* replication of any scientific research may not always be possible due to errors or differences in the environment of testing and so on.

Science and Common Sense

Science is, in many ways, a reaction to the 'common sense' approach. In fact, many of the beliefs humans have had throughout the ages have been based on common sense, and the doubts about these beliefs may well be what provoked the first primitive attempts at scientific explanation. For example, it used to be perfectly well accepted common sense that the Earth was flat and that after travelling a certain distance across it you would fall off it into space. However, through careful observation and mathematical calculation, scientists worked out that the Earth was not flat but actually a spherical ellipsoid (ask your geography teacher) and this discovery was made by Ancient Greeks long before we had the ability to travel out into space and look back at the Earth. Now this is important because many of the assumptions of religion are based on belief or what feels right – a kind of intuition about what must be.

Take, for example, the belief that many religious people have that they simply 'cannot accept the possibility that there is no divine being out there'. This would be a perfectly acceptable position in relation to the religious methods you have looked at up to this point, but definitely not for anyone using the scientific method –why? Let's look at a typical belief which people still have (not a religious one), but one that maybe even your teachers might have.

Talk Point

What things do you believe which are just 'common sense'?

The Full Moon Effect

Many people have a belief that when it's a full moon, people's behaviour will be affected. Teachers may even feel that pupils' behaviour gets worse during a full moon (ask them). Actually, some people worry so much about the effects of the full moon that they refuse to go out on such days – concerned that there might be a greater chance of coming to some harm. A group of psychologists decided to look into this matter further and see what the evidence was telling us. They analysed 37 studies in this area covering all sorts of

things: crime rates, road traffic accidents, admissions to hospitals, deaths and so on, and found that there was no increase in any of these things during the time when there was a full moon. So, the evidence seems to go against the hypothesis that the existence of a full moon causes negative behaviours ('*Much ado about the full moon*': Rotton, Cluver & Kelly 1985).

Common sense versus science is actually an important issue for the scientific method because sometimes what we see leads to **assumptions** about what follows and therefore what is. This is called the **deductive method**. Here, we assume that X leads to Y all things being equal (which they rarely are). An example might be that we look around at nature and assume that there must have been a super-powerful creator who made it all (but more of that later). However, the deductive method has some major flaws, the most serious probably being that sometimes our deductions don't match up with what we experience. For example, here is a piece of deduction which is obviously flawed:

1 Everything in the Universe is made up of atoms.

2 Atoms are invisible.

3 You are made up of atoms.

4 Therefore you must be invisible…

The solution to this problem, and so to separate common sense or simple deduction from scientific evidence is the **inductive scientific method** above.

Simple Section Summary

◆ Scientific method is simply a structured way to test out experience and observation.
◆ It involves a common set of procedures for verifying or falsifying hypotheses.
◆ Once something has been repeatedly verified it may become a scientific law.
◆ Inductive reasoning goes from general observations to testable theories to scientific laws.
◆ All findings in science are tentative – this means that they can be overturned if new evidence comes along.
◆ Science helps to support or reject our common-sense experience of the world.
◆ Deductive reasoning is a less powerful form of scientific method than inductive reasoning.

Strengths and Limitations of Scientific Method versus Common Sense

Strengths	Limitations
• Common sense is based on what we actually experience as opposed to some law which someone else has devised.	• Common sense may be particular to time and place and person – for example, it was once thought that it was 'common sense' not to allow women to take part in sports because they were somehow 'too delicate'.
• Scientific method can follow on from common sense provided that we are prepared to have our common sense explanations rejected.	• Sometimes people find it hard to be 'counter-intuitive' i.e. – if scientific method demonstrates that common sense is wrong then humans aren't always good at accepting it, for example, we know that the seasons are caused by the tilt of the Earth and so the angle at which the sun's energy strikes particular places throughout the Earth's orbit of the sun – but ask people why it's cold in winter and hot in summer (in Scotland) and some will still give answers like "it's because the Earth is further from the sun in winter"…

Strengths	Limitations
• Deductive reasoning can save us 'reinventing the wheel' every time we face a particular situation because we can deduce that if X leads to Y, then X+1 is likely to lead to Y+1 without having to test it out.	• As the 'invisible' example above shows, you can't always conclude one thing from another based on reason alone – you must go further by examining the evidence.

Source 10

Scientific Progress

Scientific development depends in part on a process of non-incremental or revolutionary change. Some revolutions are large, like those associated with the names of Copernicus, Newton, or Darwin, but most are much smaller, like the discovery of oxygen or the planet Uranus. The usual prelude to changes of this sort is, I believed, the awareness of anomaly, of an occurrence or set of occurrences that does not fit existing ways of ordering phenomena. The changes that result therefore require 'putting on a different kind of thinking-cap', one that renders the anomalous lawlike but that, in the process, also transforms the order exhibited by some other phenomena, previously unproblematic.

Comment: Kuhn is a well-known philosopher of science. Here he argues that science progresses through challenges to the accepted view of things. Such accepted views must be open to challenge and further investigation but the evidence which results might solve one problem but create a new one by challenging some other principle. This again, is what science is, uncomfortable though it might be to our settled way of seeing the world.

The Essential Tension (1977), xvii, Thomas S. Kuhn

Verifying and Falsifying

So, scientific method is based on the idea that scientists observe, hypothesise, test (or experiment) and then verify. **Verification** simply means that the evidence upholds the hypothesis. Where this is seen repeatedly, the findings may become a scientific **law**. This law will hold only as long as the evidence continues to support it. If modified experiments and research begin to cast doubt on the supporting evidence then the law might well be abandoned completely and a new law put in its place. Potentially this could go on forever and that's why science is an ongoing process. Perhaps the laws of science in a thousand years will be different to what they are now – who knows? In principle, everything according to science has to be able to be **verified** or **falsified** (falsified simply means that the evidence does not support the hypothesis). If a question cannot be verified or falsified then it is outside the scope of science. For example:

A Pink Teapot

Suppose someone claims that there is a giant pink teapot orbiting the Earth. This would be easy to verify because we could look with telescopes or use radio telescopes or use existing satellites to search for this unmistakable feature. However, the person who claims this says that he was told this in a dream by the beings who live in the teapot and that the teapot is completely invisible. Now we could still look for it because all objects of mass have a gravitational pull on the matter around them, so we should be able to measure the 'bending' of matter or light or space around this teapot. However, the person who had the dream adds that the teapot can control its gravitational effect so that it leaves no trace around it.

In short, we have no way of verifying or falsifying this person's claim about the teapot. It is now a question which is not open to scientific enquiry and so we cannot by definition provide any evidence to support or reject this person's claim. If you substitute the idea of God for the teapot you should now begin to see the difficulty of applying scientific method to religious claims.

Talk Point

11

Think of other questions which might be, in principle, unverifiable or unfalsifiable.

Strengths and Limitations of Verification and Falsification

Strengths	Limitations
• Verification requires supporting evidence and so is based on proper scientific enquiry.	• What counts as verified can be the subject of interpretation and disagreement even among scientists.
• Verification and falsification require us to devise suitable scientific tests to arrive at our conclusions.	• It is arguable that some questions are not verifiable or falsifiable and therefore outside the scope of scientific enquiry – for example, if you tried to verify the following you'd have problems: "The planet furthest from the Earth is shaped like a banana." You can't verify this or falsify it because (at the moment) you can't get there, but even if you could, unless you come up against a great barrier marked 'end of the Universe' you couldn't be completely sure that there wasn't another planet further on…
• Verification and falsification give us failsafe, reliable ways to understand the Universe.	• Perhaps humans 'need' mystery?

Sources 11 and 12

Scientific Method

The growth of our knowledge is the result of a process closely resembling what Darwin called 'natural selection'; that is, the natural selection of hypotheses: our knowledge consists, at every moment, of those hypotheses which have shown their (comparative) fitness by surviving so far in their struggle for existence, a competitive struggle which eliminates those hypotheses which are unfit.

In so far as a scientific statement speaks about reality, it must be falsifiable: and in so far as it is not falsifiable, it does not speak about reality.

Comment: Popper is one of the most famous philosophers of science. His argument here is firstly that science progresses through the modification of previously existing hypotheses. Those which stand up to the evidence survive and those which do not, don't. In the second quote he stresses his view that if a statement or theory cannot be falsified (or verified) it is unscientific.

Objective Knowledge: An Evolutionary Approach (1971), 261. Karl Raimund Popper, cited in Dean Keith Simonton, Origins of Genius: Darwinian Perspectives on Creativity (1999), 26

The Logic of Scientific Discovery (2002), 316. Karl Raimund Popper, cited at www.todayinsci.com/P/Popper_Karl/PopperKarl-Quotations.htm

Scientific Models

Science often uses **models** to help us get our heads around difficult concepts. For example, chemical substances are drawn as models which do not reflect how these things 'look' in reality. These reflect the real thing but are not: they are simply a helpful way for us to make sense of difficult concepts and ideas. Scientific models can also be **predictive** – in that scientists will input all sorts of data to make predictions about what might happen should X or Y be modified (for example, by the input of climate data into a computer programme to predict possible climate change). These predictions are not just guesswork, but attempts to use the best available evidence to reach conclusions about things which as yet cannot be directly verified (for example, it is not possible to measure future climate change due to the rather annoying fact that the future hasn't turned up yet).

Models can also be the source of deductions in science in the absence of hard evidence. For example, a model might suggest that in condition X, Y will happen. If we observe Y actually happening in condition X then we deduce that it is likely to have been caused by X according to the model we are working with. Scientific models can lead to what are called scientific **paradigms** (pronounced *paradyms*). These paradigms are models which have stood the test of time and mean that we can base our models on previous models. We can modify scientific paradigms and they can even be completely replaced with a new paradigm – as long as the evidence supports the new paradigm and rejects the previous one.

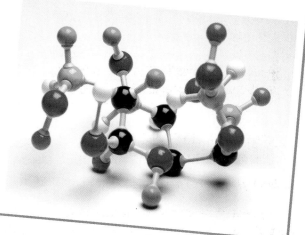

Talk Point

DNA is usually presented in the form of a model. Find an example and talk it through. Does this help us to make sense of this important structure?

Strengths and Limitations of Models

Strengths	Limitations
• Models help us to conceptualise what we otherwise couldn't.	• The model – however good – isn't the real thing, just a shadow of it.
• Models help us predict what we can't currently test.	• Such prediction is always going to be open to differences in interpretation.
• Paradigms give us a starting point for further research and are open to challenge.	• There are many cases of scientists facing extreme difficulties when challenging cherished scientific paradigms.

Scientific Objectivity

Objectivity is one of the most important principles within scientific method. Science and scientists have to test and conclude based on the evidence they uncover. If it goes against their hypothesis then so be it – even if they still have a hunch that somehow their hypothesis is right. In fact, even if it goes against a long-accepted theory or scientific law, it must be accepted. It is all about the evidence.

Now of course, this isn't always easy. It might mean the rejection of some scientist's life's work – it might mean going against people considered to be great scientists. It might mean rewriting every single science textbook in existence. It might mean being mocked and challenged and having to be a lone voice in opposition to everyone else. Some scientists have faced great personal difficulty in presenting their findings because of the challenges these findings presented to the 'scientific community'. Scientists are human after all and it isn't always easy when someone shatters everything you have lived your life thinking to be true. But, and it's a very big but, scientists should welcome this because it is after all what makes science what it is.

Science should not be about personalities or about cherished theories which are indestructible, but about responding to the evidence no matter what it seems to be saying – even if it goes against everything which has gone before (perhaps especially so). Of course this would be difficult to swallow- but if you don't, you have rejected the very principles upon which scientific method is based and it would be hard to see how you could be considered to be a scientist any more – you have probably now become a 'believer'.

Source 13

Scientific Objectivity

The scientist, Richard Dawkins gives a good example of what this scientific objectivity should mean:

For years [a respected scientist in the zoology department at Oxford University] had passionately believed, and taught, that the Golgi Apparatus (a microscopic feature of the interior of cells) was not real... Every Monday afternoon it was the custom of the whole department to listen to a talk by a visiting lecturer. One Monday, the visitor was an American cell biologist who presented completely convincing evidence that the Golgi Apparatus was real. At the end of the lecture the [respected scientist] strode to the front of the hall, shook the American by the hand and said – with passion – 'My dear fellow, I wish to thank you. I have been wrong these fifteen years.' We clapped our hands red... The memory of the incident I have described still brings a lump to my throat.

Comment: Dawkins makes clear that not all scientists might have responded like this example, but makes it equally clear that this scientist – in admitting that he had been wrong – was demonstrating the kind of objectivity which all scientists should aspire to.

The God Delusion p320–321

Talk Point 13

Why might some scientists not have responded the way the scientist in Dawkins' example did? Would you?

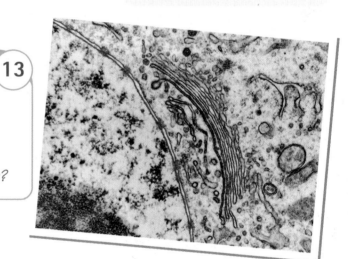

Simple Section Summary

◆ Science makes progress by challenging the accepted views of things, testing them out and suggesting new ways of seeing things based on the evidence gathered.

◆ Where the evidence supports a hypothesis the hypothesis is verified.

◆ Where it does not, the hypothesis is falsified/rejected.

◆ For something to be scientific it has to be able to be verified or falsified.

◆ Science uses models to help explain concepts and get a mental picture of them.

◆ Models can help predict what might happen if something is changed.

◆ Science should be objective – ideas should be based only on the evidence found and not a pre-existing belief.

Strengths and Limitations of Objectivity

Strengths	Limitations
• It means that your views about how the world is are based on solid evidence.	• Evidence remains open to interpretation.
• It is a fundamental principle of science that objectivity must be maintained throughout the application of scientific method. This safeguards science from being 'twisted' by people's own views.	• Scientists are human and 100% objectivity might be hard to achieve. Besides, many great scientific developments have come from scientists who followed their 'intuition' even at points where the evidence seemed to be going against them.

Scientifically Proven!

Pause for a moment and ask yourself how many TV adverts you have seen which make all sorts of claims that a product has been 'scientifically proven'. It might be that the product claims to kill 99% of all known germs or that eight out of ten hamsters prefer this hamster food to the next 'leading brand' – or, more troublesome may be that this product reverses the visible signs of ageing, or helps you lose weight on a diet of ice cream and chocolate and so on… From what you know already, you should be aware that nothing in science is ever really **proved** – all you have is the best possible match for the evidence currently available – evidence which might have to be rejected tomorrow.

However, just as in the religious method, the **interpretation** of the evidence can be very important in reaching your claims. Just as reading a bit of the Bible can lead to two very different understandings, so too can interpretation of the scientific evidence. Actually, for some people this can be a very annoying feature of the scientific method because to them it seems as if science seems to be saying one thing one week and the opposite the next week (eat no fat/eat some fat; get some exercise/don't overdo the exercise.. and so on). Science is still a human activity and so it can suffer from some of the less desirable features of human nature and so what counts as scientific proof has to be understood carefully.

Who Did the Research?

Scientists are employed. Sometimes this means that their findings can be the subject of "spin" to fit a particular end result. For example, a scientist employed by a drug company may highlight the evidence which supports the drug's effectiveness and 'play down' any contradictory evidence. The scientist is not telling lies – simply interpreting and then presenting his findings in a particular way to match his employer's needs.

What Research was Carried Out?

Sometimes the claims for a product are made in a one-minute advert. What experiments and research were carried out in order to arrive at these claims? Would you understand the research report if you read it? How **valid** and **reliable** was the research? How large was the sample group and how were they selected and so on? Was the research checked by an **independent** authority? Did the scientists involved demonstrate **bias** in their selection of the sample or in the techniques they used or in their interpretation of the results?

What Other Research is there Out There?

Perhaps the claims are based on one piece of research which is maybe contradicted by every other piece of research on the topic. You're not going to be told about this in a TV advert and it's pretty unlikely that you'll go and read all the scientific literature about a product before you go and buy it. In fact, pick a bottle of shampoo from your bathroom and look at the ingredients – have you even got the first idea about what they are and how they were put together and so – maybe importantly – what they might do to you when you slop them all over your head?

Will the Research Findings Apply to You?

Let's say that product X was 'found to work for 75 out of 80 people who used it'. Maybe you will be one of the five for whom it won't work – how will you know unless you buy the product yourself and test it out for yourself? You might just be wasting your money…

Do you use any product because it is 'scientifically proven'?
Do your parents?

Source 14

Science

"I am against religion because it teaches us to be satisfied with not understanding the world."

"Faith is the great cop-out, the great excuse to evade the need to think and evaluate evidence. Faith is belief in spite of, even perhaps because of, the lack of evidence."

Comment: Richard Dawkins is a scientist and a well-known critic of all things religious. These quotes demonstrate that for him, science is about understanding the world and this is achieved through the scientific method, based on evidence as opposed to religion which is about mystery and for Dawkins, is based on lack of evidence. For Dawkins, religion would be considered to be an example of something which has such vague, unsupported claims as to be meaningless.

Richard Dawkins at http://richarddawkins.net/quotes

Scientific Method, Religion and Human Nature

Science should be seen as much as a method as a body of knowledge. In school you may well be learning scientific theories and ideas but you should also be learning how to *do* science. It is a **practical activity** and for some people, very central to what it means to be human. Human beings have always been curious – and always will be (probably!). That curiosity has led to us trying to explain the world around us – how did it originate? Where did life 'come from'? What is our life for?

Of course, many people have arrived at 'religious' answers to these questions and many have arrived at 'scientific' answers. Of course, many have arrived at both. Whatever their conclusions, they have been reached as a result of enquiry and of interpreting the 'evidence' whether that is the results of scientific experiments or trying to work out the meaning of scriptural texts. You will come across both throughout this book… but what is the 'truth' may still be difficult to work out, but it is probably in our human nature to be forever trying to work out what the truth is. The scientist, Carl Sagan, a very dedicated Humanist, argued for the scientific method as a way of making ourselves truly human.

Source 15

The Value of Science

Finding the occasional straw of truth awash in a great ocean of confusion and bamboozle requires vigilance, dedication and courage. But if we don't practise these tough habits of thought, we cannot hope to solve the truly serious problems that face us and we risk becoming a nation of suckers, a world of suckers, up for grabs by the next charlatan who saunters along

Comment: Sagan argues that throughout history, humanity has been open to being fooled by all sorts of things (including credible charlatans). It is only really science and the practise of science which will help us avoid this and so find our own way as a species.

Carl Sagan: The Demon-Haunted World, Science as a Candle in the Dark p42

Strengths and Limitations of Scientific Method Summarised

Strengths	Limitations
• Scientific method, in whatever form, is based on rigorous, methodical approaches where the 'truth' is based on the best evidence available.	• Scientific method is subject to a number of possible flaws which could lead to the evidence being inaccurate, incomplete or interpreted in such ways so as to support an already existing point of view. In science the view/belief should follow as a result of the evidence – sometimes it's the opposite.

Strengths	Limitations
• Such evidence by definition is open to challenge, change and modification if superior evidence comes along.	• Interpretation of evidence is always an issue in science and can lead to competing and confusing claims. In addition, scientists are not as open to modifying evidence as they would like to appear to be.
• Science is therefore the most reliable way of explaining the world around us and our place in it.	• Science is limited in what it can explain. There may be some questions which are not possible to investigate using any form of scientific method.

Activities

Knowledge, Understanding, Analysis and Evaluation

1 Explain how Little Red Riding Hood (Agnes) used the scientific method.

2 Explain the following terms: observation; data; hypothesis; verification; falsification; generalisation; prediction; law (scientific); theory; replication.

3 What is meant by inductive reasoning?

4 Is inductive reasoning 100% foolproof? Explain your answer.

5 Describe one strength and one limitation of inductive reasoning.

6 Why is it inaccurate to say that science *proves* things?

7 What are scientific theories based upon?

8 Give an example of a common sense belief.

9 Explain how science has rejected one 'common sense belief'.

10 What is the full moon effect and what has the evidence shown about it?

11 Explain the difference between the inductive and the deductive method in science.

12 Describe one limitation of the deductive method.

13 What argument does Kuhn propose about scientific change?

14 Is an unfalsifiable statement open to scientific investigation? Explain your answer.

15 Can science investigate everything? Explain your answer.

16 Popper compared scientific theories to 'survival of the fittest'. What did he mean?

17 In what ways does science use models? What are the advantages and disadvantages of using such models?

18 What is scientific objectivity?

19 Is complete scientific objectivity possible? Explain your answer.

20 What questions should you ask about a product which is 'scientifically proven'?

21 Do these questions relate to all scientific claims? Explain your answer.

22 Describe your own experience of science in school. Are you learning about it, to do it or both? (No comments about any science teachers please...)

23 Carl Sagan argues that science is what stops the world becoming a place full of suckers. What does he mean? Do you agree?

24 Explain one strength and one limitation of scientific method.

Active Learning

1 Find another fairy tale. Now examine it for evidence that the scientific method has been used.

2 Here are some scientific hypotheses. Explain how you might use scientific method to support or reject these hypotheses:

- Blondes are more intelligent than brunettes.

- Watching TV violence makes you aggressive.

- Behaviour in your school deteriorates during the time of the full moon.

- Pupils perform academically more poorly on Tuesdays than on Thursdays.

- Irn Bru makes you brainy.

- You can tell the difference between Coke and Pepsi in a blind taste test.

NB: If you decide to carry out any of these pieces of research make sure that you take advice from an experienced researcher (perhaps a science or psychology teacher). This is because it is very important to safeguard anyone or anything you do such research with. As you're studying RMPS, I assume you might not know about the rules

associated with scientific research (and your teacher might not either). To be on the safe side, it might just be best to write what you would do but not actually do it!

3 Think up some other hypotheses which could be researched in the same way.

4 Find out about some scientific theories which have been replaced with others and produce an information leaflet/display about them – some ideas are:

- Flat Earth
- Sun going round the Earth
- Lightning coming from the gods

5 Discuss and come up with some hypotheses which are unverifiable.

6 Write a magazine article about the possibility that an invisible, undiscoverable giant pink teapot is orbiting the Earth. Include some (made up) quotes from scientists about this possibility (or impossibility).

7 Do some research into the kinds of things scientists might model. What are the benefits and drawbacks of such models?

8 Record some TV adverts or find some magazine adverts which make claims about being 'scientifically proven'. What evidence is presented? What questions should be asked? You could have a look at the product's website if one exists and see what further detail is made available. How reliable are the claims? Present your findings to your class.

9 Some things in life are referred to as 'pseudoscience'. These are things which have, on the surface, scientific credibility, but which more 'traditional' scientists can be very critical about (sometimes in a very hostile way!). Create a display or give a presentation on your findings. What does this tell you about the scientific method, scientists or those who claim to have scientific support. Some examples for you to use might be:

- Neuro-Linguistic Programming (NLP)

- Homeopathy

- Astrology

Unit Assessment Question

Higher:
'Scientific method is the only reliable way to uncover the truth.' To what extent do you agree? **KU8 AE4**

Intermediate 2:
Explain one strength and one limitation of scientific method. **AE4**

Sample Exam Question

Higher:
Explain two of the limitations of scientific method. **AE4**

Intermediate 2:
'In science, a hypothesis must be falsifiable.' What does this statement mean? **KU4**

Homework

Find out about the lives and work of either Karl Popper or Thomas Kuhn. What were their views about science? Write a short report on your findings.

Personal Reflection

In your own life, how important is it to have evidence for the things you believe or for the way you live your life? How many things do you believe in which have little or no evidence, or where the evidence is inconclusive? What things in your life could you put through the principles of scientific method? Would you want to?

It's a late night talk show called Ivory Towers which has regular guests who are at the top of their fields of study. The show has previously included doctors, lawyers, entrepreneurs – all world-class, well-known, and at the cutting edge of their particular disciplines. Previous guests have included Dr Crick, the scientist who discovered DNA, the founder of Microsoft, Bill Gates, and of course Simon Cowell. Tonight's programme is a discussion between the nuclear physicist Professor Thomas Accrington-Stanley, the scientist who discovered the process by which we can now produce limitless nuclear energy using only mobile phone signals, and the Very Very Reverend Dr Bill Gordon, former Modulator of the Church of Britain – in effect, the head of all Britain's Christians. Tonight's show, hosted by Jerome Poodle is entitled: 'Science, the new religion?'

Jerome: Good evening and welcome to *Ivory Towers*. I have with me tonight two of the world's best-known figures from the worlds of science and religion: Professor Thomas Accrington-Stanley, Head of Nuclear Physics at the Oban Institute of Technology and The Very Very Reverend Doctor Bill Gordon, Modulator of the Church of Britain. Tonight we'll be discussing whether science has replaced religion as a new faith. This is in light of yesterday's survey published by Gollop, which claims that many of the UK population no longer believes in God, and also don't understand basic science. Dr Gordon, is God still there?

Bill: Of course he is. His wonders are all around us to behold. We just have to listen for him.

→

Thomas: *(cups his hand to his ear)* Don't hear him, but hang on... I think I hear some fairies at the bottom of the garden chortling away...

Bill: You would. That's because you're really silly.

Thomas: Silly am I? I'm not the one who has to believe in a big man in the sky because I'm scared to go to sleep without my night-light on.

Bill: Well you've never grown out of playing with your train sets and watching Star Trek – that's why. Oh, and how's the trainspotting coming on?

Thomas: Those numbers mean something you know.

Bill: No they don't. You're just a sad little man playing with your test tubes and machines. God'll get you back you know.

Thomas: Let him try, I'll zap him with my newly devised ray gun.

Bill: If you do, I'll tell my mum on you.

Jerome: *(has been looking more horrified and puzzled as the 'debate' has gone on)* So, eh, gentlemen, erm, is it your opinion that science has replaced religion?

Thomas: *(points at Bill)* Yes, it has. You lose! *(In a sing-song style)* Na-na-na-na-na – I'm smarter than you-oo.

Bill: *(childishly)* God's going to strike you down, and smash all your test tubes and break your thermometers.

Thomas: I'm a physicist you twit.

Bill: Well, he'll make your oscilloscope go funny.

Thomas: He'd have to exist first.

Bill: He does!

Thomas: Doesn't.

Bill: Does, does, does.

Thomas: Doesn't, doesn't doesn't, doesn't , doesn't, doesn't doesn't... so there. *(folds his arms and turns his back on Bill)*

Bill: I'm going to get my big brother on you, he'll sort out all you smelly old scientists.

Thomas: *(back still turned)* I'll get my big brother, cos' he's bigger than yours and he'll fix all you boring religious people.

Jerome: *(bewildered)* Well gentlemen, I'm afraid that's all we've got time for at the moment. Thank you for your contributions and it's goodnight from Dr Gordon.

Bill: *(sulkily)* Nighty night.

Jerome: And it's goodnight from Professor Accrington-Stanley.

Thomas: *(back turned)* Humph...

Jerome: And it's goodnight from me, goodnight...

The Relationship between Science and Religion

It really is just as well that scientists and religious people don't communicate like that, although throughout the history of the debates between science and religion, it has sometimes come quite close, with a famous debate over evolution in 1860 between Bishop Wilberforce and TH Huxley, a supporter of the new evolutionary theory, where Wilberforce asked whether Huxley's ancestors were apes on his grandmother's or grandfather's side. To set the scene for the debates between religion and science, here's a very brief history of their relationship throughout the ages. This history refers to the relationship between science and religion in the western world.

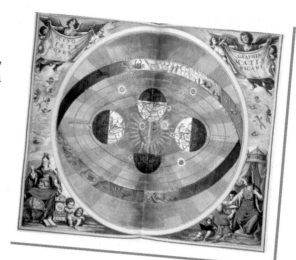

A Very Brief History of Science and Religion

- In the ancient world, belief in the **gods** was taken for granted. Humans were their playthings, and all things in nature were under their command. They had to be kept pleased through **sacrifices** and **ceremonies**. The explanation for everything in nature was that it was created and maintained through the power of the gods.

- In some cultures, **monotheism** arose: a belief in one supreme God who eventually replaced other forms of religion. This was the case in the monotheistic Judaeo-Christian tradition which is the basis for the dominant western view of religion today.

- There were probably always people who asked scientific questions, but generally their answers were framed in such a way as to support the creative power of a God or the gods.

- The Ancient Greeks took science to a new level, and still many of our basic scientific principles today are based on the scientific discoveries of these ancient Greeks, such as Euclid and Pythagoras and so on.

- In the western world, Europe spent some time in what are referred to as the 'dark ages' here – science, to some extent, went on hold, and there was a fine line between what we'd now call science and practices such as astrology and alchemy. Fortunately, the Muslim world was keeping the science of the Ancient Greeks alive through such things as Algebra (words like this and ones like Alkaline show an Arabic origin). Eventually these ideas made their way back into the wider western world.

◆ In the Medieval period, scientific enquiry took off again, very often led by religious people who were keen to 'uncover' God's work in the Universe. Still, however, the Christian Church kept a careful eye on what scientists came up with. Anything which contradicted Church teaching would have a hard time. Scientists such as **Copernicus** and **Galileo** came into conflict with the Church because their findings contradicted the teachings of the Church. This was at a time when the Church was all-powerful and saw itself as God's representative on Earth. Many scientists suffered at the hands of the Church.

◆ In the 16th through to the 18th Centuries, **the Enlightenment** was on the go throughout Europe. In many fields, there were important scientific developments and many of the things which were formerly explained by the Church now had scientific explanations. Increasingly, science and the Church went head-to-head over issues such as the creation of the Universe in six days, the belief that the Earth was the centre of the Universe and so on. More and more, beliefs based on Church teaching and argument alone were becoming challenged by 'beliefs' based on reason and evidence.

◆ This rumbled on until some of the discoveries of the 19th century really shook things up. Some of the central beliefs of Christianity were challenged by findings in geology where the evidence seemed to suggest that the Earth was much older than the Church taught. All of this culminated in **Darwin's theory of evolution** – a direct challenge to the Church's teaching that God created everything as it is today.

◆ In the 20th Century, the discovery of **DNA**, theories in **quantum physics** and rapid advances in almost every conceivable branch of science – including the ability to clone and therefore effectively create living things – has moved scientific thinking on at great speed and often challenging further the claims of religions.

Talk Point 15

Discuss in class – what do you understand by evolutionary theory and quantum physics. What challenges do these present for religious people and how do religious people respond to them?

Throughout all of this it should be remembered that ordinary people who were not scientists or theologians had to depend on things being explained to them. This is no different today and is one of the reasons why this whole area is so complicated. The science is complex, but also the subtle religious points can be quite complex too. Both areas need to be explained in terms that ordinary people can understand so they can make up their own minds. It is probably true that even today, many people have only a vague understanding of evolutionary theory or even a superficial knowledge of basic theological ideas.

Debating the Methods – What's at Stake?

This section will examine the relationship between scientific method and the religious method we have examined so far. Specific issues will be covered in Areas 2 and 3. You should remember that these issues can produce strong emotions and sharp debate. You must always bear in mind when looking up further information (either in books or on the internet) that people can have strong views on these topics, and sometimes present their case in a clever way which can see balance and objectivity go out the window. In short, you're unlikely to come across many "Professor Accrington-Stanleys" or "Very very Reverend Dr Bill Gordons", but it's possible. For the people who engage in these debates, this is something which is absolutely crucial to their whole understanding of the world and our place in it and they see it as their 'mission' in life to get their point across – so helping humans be all they can be. For both 'sides' of the argument, what is at stake is nothing less than human nature and the future of everything. Here's a simplification outlining two extremes.

Science is Right, Religion is Wrong

◆ There is no God, we're on our own.

◆ The only way to better our lives, and so better the whole human condition, is through the application of scientific discoveries.

◆ Meaning in life comes from human independence, and becoming fulfilled as humans through human endeavour.

◆ Religion is a dangerous superstition which we should have 'grown out of' and which holds human progress back.

Religion is Right, Science is Wrong

◆ God exists, and it is through him that our lives will be fulfilled.

◆ The only way to improve our lives is through faith in God.

◆ Meaning in life comes from faith and from living a life which is pleasing to God so that we can become what he wants us to.

◆ Science is a dangerous endeavour which makes us think we are Gods and holds us back from God because it makes us think we can cope without him.

Now these are extreme views and it would be hard to identify how many people in the world might hold them, but there will be some. Such people are just as likely to have loads of academic qualifications as to be people without any. Sometimes the arguments of extreme views like these are backed up with what seem to ordinary people to be completely water-tight evidence or reasonable views. The task in this section of the course is to try to steer a course which explains these extreme viewpoints as well as some of the many viewpoints between them… ready?

Science and Religion

Science can purify religion from error and superstition; religion can purify science from idolatry and false absolutes. Each can draw the other into a wider world, a world in which both can flourish…. such bridging ministries must be nurtured and encouraged.

Pope John Paul II quoted in Carl Sagan: Billions and Billions p142

Talk Point

Discuss in class: 'Now that we have science, there is no need for religion.'

Relationship 1: The Rejection of Scientific Enquiry as a Reliable Source of Human Understanding: Literalists

At the most extreme end of the spectrum would be a Christian who rejected everything that science claims. In fact, some may even see science as coming from the **Devil** – something which gives humans a sense that we ourselves are Gods and so something which can lead to us rejecting God. Such people might reject any scientific development as going against **God's will** and therefore something to be very wary of. Their argument might well be propped up by some of the more extreme uses (in some people's opinion, abuses) of science. For example, the creation of nuclear weapons and other weapons of mass destruction, the cloning of living things, the scientific manipulation of embryo material, the recent pregnancy of a 'man', the transplantation of animal tissue into humans, the altering of the DNA of one species by merging it with the DNA of another. All of these suggest that the logical end of scientific development is that we make ourselves Gods. Of course, if we do that, then there might not be any need to believe in any other God.

Such a view is very extreme of course, and there are more moderate versions of it. Some Christian literalists might accept some of the developments of science as ways which clearly make life better for people. They could argue that science is simply us using our God-given brains to improve our lives and those of others around us. For example, if you have a

headache, you take a paracetamol – this isn't **playing God**, it's just using what God has given us to make life better. Such people might not argue that all science is some kind of demonic possession or something sent to turn us away from God, it is simply a practice which we can engage in which has no implications for religious belief. However, such people could remain convinced that scientific method is not the correct way to understand the Universe or our place in it, and its power could turn us away from being all that we can be as God's creation. Such literalists take religious claims literally – in other words, as they're written or otherwise sent by God – without any need for examination, testing and supporting with scientifically credible evidence.

Literalist views come, generally speaking, in two forms: one of which is their own argument about the validity of the religious method and the other concerns the invalidity of scientific method.

Source 17

Christian Literalists on Science

My thesis is that the disciplines find their completion in Christ and cannot be properly understood apart from Christ... The point to understand here is that Christ is never an addendum to a scientific theory but always the completion.

Comment: William A Dembski is a supporter of 'Intelligent Design'. This is a Christian position which argues that the scientific evidence exists to support the view that God created the Universe as written in the Bible. In this quote Dembski basically argues that scientific theory can reveal the person of Jesus and therefore God.

William A Dembski, Intelligent Design: The Bridge between Science and Theology,
pp 206–207

Literalists: Religious Method is Valid

The argument here is fairly simple. The religious method is the most valid and reliable way to understand what God wants, and so is the best way to work out what human life is for and therefore understand the meaning of your life and your place in the Universe. Let's look again at the religious method through the eyes of a literalist:

◆ **Revelation** of God's nature: For the literalist, the revelation of God in history is literally true. The creation story happened just as written, as did the flood, the creation of Adam and Eve, the story of Samson and so on. None of these are **myths** or just stories with a meaning. God is not an idea – he is a real being who did what the Bible says he did. What the Bible teaches about God is literally true. Jesus was not just a good teacher or a clever man. He was God made flesh, part human, part God, and his life is an example of the kind of person God is as well as the kind of person he wants us to be. God's **Holy Spirit** came down after Jesus rose from the dead and lives among us guiding us in the way that

God wants. All of this means that if science points to something which contradicts the nature of God it can be ignored because it is wrong. God has shown us who he is. Science cannot contradict that.

◆ The Scriptures are literally true in every respect and every word. They are God's word – quite literally. They do not need complex interpretation – they are just to be accepted. If it's not entirely clear what is meant then we should simply accept that as a mystery and realise that we aren't God and therefore there may be some things which we won't understand. God will make it clear to us when he chooses to. We simply need to accept that scriptures have come direct from God and that he would not include anything in them which was wrong or meaningless. So, if science contradicts scripture, we can ignore that because scripture is never wrong. Such contradictions must just mean that science has got it wrong.

◆ God does reveal himself to people through religious experience in visions, dreams, through speaking to them and so on. These are completely valid and come from God. They are not hallucinations or anything like that. God is the creator of the Universe – so appearing to us in a dream is not exactly difficult for him. We should simply accept that these experiences are real, listen to what they are telling us and act upon that advice. If science makes claims that religious experience is something other than a gift from God, then it is simply wrong.

◆ Some Christian literalists believe that God's revelation through the Church is absolutely valid in every respect. God has chosen Church leaders and guides his church – so what it says should be followed to the letter. Again, if scientific findings contradict the teachings of the Church through its leaders (appointed by God) then science is wrong and the Church right.

◆ Nature points to the existence of a creator. The vastness, order and beauty of nature could only have come about through the creative act of an all-powerful divine being. Besides, this is what the Bible says happened therefore it did. If science claims otherwise then it is wrong.

◆ Literalists argue that Christianity is about faith. That means that you just accept what the Bible says as being literally true, and you accept anything which you think has come from God. Importantly, literalists would be keen to stress that their approach is not a 'blind' one. It is based on an open approach to God's message as he has sent it, but not one without checks in place. For example, say such a literalist heard a voice from God telling him to commit a murder in God's name. Being a literalist doesn't mean that you just go out and do so right away, acting in blind faith –

you would check such an instruction with God's revelation in scripture, with the teachings of the church and so on. Being a literalist doesn't mean that you throw your brain away – it simply means that your first explanation of everything is based on your belief in the validity of the Bible and God's message sent to humans through other means.

Simple Section Summary

◆ **We should not talk about science proving things. It simply supports or rejects hypotheses.**
◆ **All scientific evidence needs to be interpreted.**
◆ **This interpretation should be done objectively.**
◆ **Research should be valid i.e. the correct methods should be used for the context.**
◆ **Research should be reliable i.e. if methods are reliable then they should give more or less the same results over time.**
◆ **Science is a body of knowledge as well as a practical activity.**
◆ **Scientific materialists argue that science is the best way to help us understand the Universe and our place in it.**

Literalists: Scientific Method is Invalid

For a literalist, the scientific method could, and would be, criticised – where it results in teachings which contradict religious beliefs. The basis of a literalist's criticism could include:

◆ Scientists base their method on **observation**, but observation requires **interpretation**. No matter how you look at it, there's always a human element to observation which is probably based on already-existing belief. For example, you might only look for an alternative explanation for the existence of human life on Earth if you already had doubts about the creation story in the Bible. Also, how you explain what you observe is still closely tied to the kind of person you are which includes your upbringing and the time and place in which you live. Drawing conclusions from observations still involves using our human intellect. According to a literalist this would be dangerous because we are '**fallen**' creatures (according to the creation story in Genesis) therefore our interpretation of what we observe is based on a flawed human nature to begin with, so the conclusions we reach must be in doubt.

◆ Similarly, hypotheses involve an element of **intuition** and sometimes a leap of **imagination**. Why choose one hypothesis over another? Perhaps by selecting one hypothesis over another and carrying out appropriate research we influence the possible outcomes we can arrive at – in other words our answers will be partly determined by the questions we ask.

◆ Research is full of **subjectivity** instead of the (impossible to achieve) **objectivity** which scientists claim it is. We may think that we are faithfully allowing the evidence to tell its story, but we may not be. Instead we may be 'reading' the evidence in light of what we already believe or think to be the case. Our choice of research methods, who or what to include/exclude, the materials we use, the statistical tests we employ to analyse our data. All of these can lead to one conclusion being arrived at rather than another. Perhaps, maybe without even knowing it, scientists arrive at conclusions which contradict religious teachings because that's what they believed in the first place – they just noticed the evidence which supported their already existing belief and ignored the evidence which contradicted it.

◆ All scientific method is based on **assumptions** (or speculations). If these assumptions are wrong then the findings which follow based upon them are wrong too. If you are carrying out research based on the assumption that life evolved then if evolution turns out to be untrue then your conclusion will be invalid. Assumptions can also be based on what seems likely. For example, there is no evidence to suggest what sounds dinosaurs would have made so scientists have speculated that what they know about the animals' size, vocal chord arrangement and so on must indicate the kind of noises they might have made. The roar of the Tyrannosaurus Rex might just as easily have been a pitiful squeal.

◆ Many elements of scientific method depend upon **evidence** which is not yet or not completely available. This means that conclusions can often be provisional upon the arrival of a suitable technique or the 'missing link' in a theory. Scientists accept this as part of the process of scientific enquiry. For a literalist this is a weakness of scientific method because it involves holding on to theories and ideas in anticipation of evidence which is not there yet.

◆ Scientific method is therefore often based on '**circumstantial** evidence' i.e. if X then Y, because there can be no other *scientifically credible* explanation. However, this is not the same statement as saying that there is observable evidence that if X then Y.

◆ Literalists also argue, crucially, that scientific method is **limited** in what it can and cannot explain. Not all things are verifiable or falsifiable and therefore are outwith the **scope** of scientific enquiry. For example, all things spiritual are not measurable using scientific techniques, so here scientific method can say very little. Spiritual things can therefore only be understood from a religious perspective and they show conclusively that scientific method has

quite profound limitations when it comes to religious matters. Besides which, science cannot answer questions such as 'is it right to kill?' for answers to these questions, literalists argue, we should turn to faith.

In summary, literalists argue that scientific enquiry as a method of developing human understanding is so full of **flaws**, theoretical and practical, that it must be rejected. Besides which, using the techniques of religious method is more than enough to help humans make sense of the world around them and our place in it.

Talk Point 17

Should we abandon science because it isn't perfect?
(Or religion for that matter...)

Simple Section Summary

- ◆ Science and religion have had a complex history.
- ◆ Both seek to explain the world but both use different methods for doing so
- ◆ Sometimes these differences have led to conflict.
- ◆ Most ordinary people probably have only a little understanding of complex science or theology.
- ◆ Scientific materialists argue that humans have to understand their Universe as they have to work out their own problems and solutions.
- ◆ They argue that meaning in life comes from our own actions.
- ◆ Religious people believe that God gives meaning to life.
- ◆ Some religious people believe that science is anti-religion.
- ◆ They argue that the negative side of science shows that it is a power which humans can't handle.
- ◆ Science, for many religious people, makes humans think they are God – this is bad
- ◆ Christian literalists believe that religious ways of finding the truth (and meaning) are the only valid ones.
- ◆ Christian literalists believe that every word of the Bible is literally true and that God does reveal himself directly to people.
- ◆ Christian literalists argue that scientific method is so full of flaws that we should be wary of it.
- ◆ For example, science can be subjective and depend upon the interpretation of a scientist who already doesn't believe in God.
- ◆ Christian literalists think that a lot of scientific findings are circumstantial – they lack real evidence.
- ◆ Interpretations, assumptions, leaps of logic and subjectivity might all weaken scientific method.

Relationship 2: The Rejection of Revelation as a Reliable Source of Human Understanding: Scientific Materialists

Source 18

Science and Religion Working Together?

You are a literalist interpreter of Christian Holy Scripture. You reject the conclusion of science that mankind evolved from lower forms. You believe that each person's soul is immortal, making this planet a way station to a second, eternal life. Salvation is assured those who are redeemed in Christ.

I am a secular humanist. I think existence is what we make of it as individuals. There is no guarantee of life after death, and heaven and hell are what we create for ourselves, on this planet. There is no other home. Humanity originated here by evolution from lower forms over millions of years. And yes, I will speak plain, our ancestors were apelike animals. The human species has adapted physically and mentally to life on Earth and no place else. Ethics is the code of behaviour we share on the basis of reason, law, honour, and an inborn sense of decency, even as some ascribe it to God's will.

Comment: EO Wilson, a former Christian and now secular humanist, in his letter to a Southern Baptist Minister. While he rejects the methods and conclusions of religion, he points out and explains what are, for him, the differences between science and religion – but hopes that they can work together to save life on Earth.

EO Wilson, http://www.conservationmagazine.org/articles/v7n4/books-19/

Again, there will be extreme views among scientific materialists. Some may well argue that religion is more than a harmless delusion, it is a dangerous one. One which has held human progress back throughout our history, been the cause of many undesirable episodes in human history and something which still keeps the world living in the dark when an alternative life based on the findings of science brings us out into the light as a species and makes the future bright, unshackled from the chains of religious **dogma** and **superstition.**

Such extreme views may argue that religious people are at best fooling themselves and at worst believing in something which gives them some kind of power or hold over ordinary people, through guilt and fear and worry about eternal punishments and so on. They might argue that such people stand in the way of scientific progress and would have us all return to the dark ages where, instead of seeking cures to illness and disease through scientific enquiry, we will sit around waiting for a non-existent God to cure us through some kind of spiritual power (bearing in mind that as creator he must have sent the illness or disease in the first place). Such scientists might argue that religious literalists are confused about their responses to scientific developments – for example by questioning genetic engineering as 'playing God' while being quite happy to 'play God' by interfering in his great plan to give you a headache by taking a paracetamol.

A scientific extremist might well argue that religious literalists leave their brains behind when discussing both scientific issues and religious ones. In fact, a scientific materialist might argue that religion is something which, rather than helping us become who we are, actually stands in the way of humans becoming all that they can be and as such is a dangerous and needless **delusion** which requires to be cured. There are some scientific materialists who might argue that while religion is wrong, it's harmless enough – no worse than having any other kind of imaginary friend. Again, let's examine how scientific literalists support scientific method and then explore their criticisms of religious method.

Scientific Materialists: Scientific Method is Valid

Again, it's a simple enough argument. Scientific method isn't perfect, but it's the best method we have for uncovering the secrets of the Universe. As such, it is in fact the noblest human endeavour and something which points to the fact that we are growing up as a species, and not remaining dependent on some divine father-figure like helpless children.

◆ **Observation** is interpreted but such interpretation isn't just based on individual scientist's whims. The whole scientific method is subject to very strict **rules** which are safeguarded by the **scientific community** worldwide. Anyone can test out a scientist's claims and discuss and argue with his findings. We interpret what we observe all the time, but science does this in a careful systematic, planned and organised way. The same method is applied throughout the scientific community as opposed to the religious 'method' which has all sorts of varieties depending upon the faith you follow or the version of it you follow in a particular time and place. In science, your interpretation of what you observe can be tested again and again by others using the same method – so your observation can be verified or falsified over and over again thus leading to scientific progress.

◆ **Hypotheses** are not randomly generated. They draw upon the whole community of scientific knowledge throughout the ages. Of course science involves a leap of imagination – or rather the investigation of things which have arisen through curiosity, but the major difference here is that the hypotheses are open to rejection through the **accumulation of evidence**. Scientists welcome the rejection of their hypotheses just as much as they welcome these hypotheses being supported.

◆ Research is as **objectively** carried out as it is possible to do. Scientists are well aware of the dangers of subjectivity and of becoming so close to your research that you start finding the answers you want to find. That's why methods such as **single** and **double blind** techniques as well as **randomisation of variables** and **peer-validation** are so important. Scientific method is not a tool to prop up a particular scientist's belief – it is a way to uncover the evidence and the evidence is all – even if the evidence goes against everything that the scientist (or scientific community) expected to be the case.

◆ Science only enquires into things which are, in principle, **verifiable** or **falsifiable**. This is a strength, not a weakness. Science only claims to be true that which it has observed in evidence, and its 'truths' are always **provisional** – they can be rejected if better evidence comes along. Science is also incremental in how it builds up its picture of the Universe. Links between scientific findings may not be clear right away, but links across scientific disciplines often produce new findings which no one expected to be the case and which aid scientific progress.

◆ Certainly, science makes assumptions sometimes without the evidence being there or with some 'missing links', but in this case science does not claim that its findings are truths – just hypotheses awaiting verification or falsification should the technique or information become available. Therefore, anything which is not supported by evidence is a theory and even things supported by evidence – even pretty solid evidence- are always open to question and revision.

◆ To argue that because scientific method is limited in what it can explain is a little like blaming a footballer for not being able to swim butterfly while on the football field. Science makes scientific claims based on scientific evidence. Scientific method is the best available way for the human species to make sense of the Universe and our place in it.

◆ In summary, scientific method is not just a body of beliefs. It is a method through which scientists test and re-test hypotheses and is always open to challenge and change.

Scientific Materialists: Religious Method is Invalid

Most scientific materialists would probably argue that religious 'method' is nothing like a method in the sense that a scientific method is. However, they might criticise religious method on the following grounds:

◆ The argument that God has revealed himself is based on historical events or current experiences which are not open to **scientific enquiry**. It could well be asked for example, why God was so often physically present throughout the Christian Old Testament, but then reduced his personal appearances in number and drama as the Bible progresses through history. Also, the God of the Christian Old Testament seems quite different to the God of the New Testament as well as to the much more open-minded God which seems to be the message coming from Christians today. The God of the Old Testament for example, seems to be easily annoyed and quick to punish and perhaps occasionally a little confused about exactly what he wants. If religious method means working out God's nature from his Biblical appearances, exactly what kind of God are we talking about?

◆ You would have a difficult job in defending the Bible as a source of scientific knowledge (though many Christians do). Apart from its obvious **contradictions**, it is also full of scientific inaccuracy – for example that the fish's digestive tract didn't dissolve Jonah. The Bible also makes no mention of the fact that the vast majority of species which have ever lived on Earth are now extinct – what's going on? Did God create things and then, realising he'd made some mistakes, rub them out and start all over again? The Bible is a document written by humans from a particular time-period with particular issues in mind. It should not be treated as a reliable source of human understanding because these writers knew only about their own world not the future, and they were not scientists so they could not write meaningfully about scientific issues. Religious people often argue that the Bible has to be interpreted intelligently, but that would involve the very interpretation which literalists would criticise scientists for. If you start to treat the Bible as sometimes true and sometimes not, how do you decide which is which? Seeking to understand the modern world through using an old book is really not a very effective way for humans to make sense of what's around them.

◆ Focusing on the life and teachings of one man in the person of **Jesus** is really very difficult to swallow. While his teachings might have good points, it would seem very strange for a whole world to base its beliefs on him for evermore – besides which most people on the planet don't – and they don't seem to have empty, directionless lives in any way. Also, the Jesus story is so full of later **amendments** and **editing** that it would be hard for anyone to claim that what's in the Bible is a particularly reliable version of who Jesus was and what he did. Also, there are the **supernatural** aspects of Jesus. Why were they necessary? Why did God need to break his own laws of nature to show who he was? Basing your understanding of life, the Universe and everything on such 'revelations' is just too complex to be in any way meaningful.

◆ The Christian Church is hardly a good example of the revelation of God. It could be argued that the Church has changed it's views on things so many times that it's difficult to see how it can be a revelation form God (or perhaps that God is revealing that he's not really very sure about X or Y). Also, the Christian church today is so divided and separated out into a staggering number of **sects** and groups – all claiming to follow God's way – which one is right? Which one reveals God's will?

◆ Religious experience as a revelation from God is just so debatable. 'Religious experiences' can be brought on by drugs or illness or stimulation of the temporal lobes or brain injury, or suggestion or expectation or lack of oxygen or tiredness, stress and on and on it goes. Why do some people have religious experiences and others do not? There are many cases of people who live pretty horrible lives who have a religious experience which changes their life right enough, but also there are many, many more who do not have any direct experience of God. Also, there are people who live good religious lives and would love to have a religious experience but just don't, often leading to them losing their faith and giving up their religion. Also, there are some who have religious experiences which lead to them doing quite ungodly kinds of things No, religious experience as a revelation from God is just far too questionable. And besides, it is 'evidence' only for the people who have them: it is neither verifiable nor falsifiable.

◆ Believing in God based upon your experience of the awe and wonder of nature is also very dubious. Nature may look beautiful and ordered, but it's not. Nature is violent and ugly. It involves a **struggle** for survival. Look more closely at a beautiful field of flowers – you'll see insects eating each other, bacteria devouring the dead, one plant straining to block out the sunlight for another so it survives and the other doesn't. The life of every living thing on Earth (more or less) depends upon the death of another. What is this telling us about God? That he is unpredictable? Random? Likes a winner? Enjoys the struggle? If the religious method means God revealing himself through nature then what he's revealing is a character that doesn't seem particularly nice.

So, is it all hopeless? Are religious people and scientists always going to be on opposite sides battling it out? Obviously not, because many people are both religious people as well as accepting the findings of science, and there are scientists who are also religious people. Perhaps there is a middle way.

Talk Point 18

Does everything in life require scientific 'proof'? Are there some things which don't?

Simple Section Summary

◆ Some scientific materialists think religion is a harmless enough thing.
◆ Others think that it is a dangerous delusion.
◆ Scientific materialists may argue that religion holds humans back in their understanding by making us accept things without testing them out.
◆ Scientific materialists argue that scientific method is as valid and reliable as it can be and so is the best way of working out what is true.
◆ For example, subjectivity and assumptions are not completely unregulated – the whole scientific community keeps a check on these kinds of things.
◆ At least scientific method is based on evidence which, scientific materialists say, is better than blind belief.
◆ Scientific materialists argue that because religion is not open to question it is not as valuable as scientific method.
◆ For example, contradictions and illogical things in the Bible suggest it is just a story book.
◆ Also, too much of religious method is far too subjective, like religious experiences. This means that it cannot be tested and so is worth little.
◆ The revelation of God either in nature, the Bible or human life, according to scientific materialists, is confusing, contradictory and unclear, so is of little value.

Relationship 3: The Acceptance of Both Revelation and Scientific Enquiry as Reliable Sources of Human Understanding

However, many scientists remain fully committed religious people and many religious people are quite happy to accept the theories and methods of science alongside their religious beliefs. Are such people simply living with some kind of split personality where they can switch one method of thinking off and engage in another – or is there something else going on? Is it possible for religion and science to live side by side? For some, as you have seen the simple answer is no, but for others their own interpretation of their own 'method' leads them to the conclusion that it is quite acceptable to have religious beliefs while explaining the Universe through scientific means.

Sources 19 and 20

Non-overlapping Magisteria

I believe, with all my heart, in a respectful, even loving concordat between the magisteria of science and religion – the NOMA concept. NOMA represents a principled position on moral and intellectual grounds, not a merely diplomatic solution. NOMA also cuts both ways. If religion can no longer dictate the nature of factual conclusions residing properly within the magisterium of science, then scientists cannot claim higher insight into moral truth from any superior knowledge of the world's empirical constitution. This mutual humility leads to important practical consequences in a world of such diverse passions. We would do well to embrace the principle and enjoy the consequences.

Comment: Gould was both a professor of Zoology and Geology at Harvard University in the USA. He argues that science and religion occupy different 'fields' or magisteria where science, 'defines the natural world' and religion 'defines our moral world'. He argues therefore that 'their spheres of influence are separate. Basically this means that he is arguing that science answers scientific questions and religion answers religious ones. They should not stray into each others' territory.

Responding to NOMA

It is a tedious cliché (and unlike many clichés it isn't even true) that science concerns itself with how questions but only theology is equipped to answer why questions. What on Earth is a why question? ... Perhaps there are some genuinely profound and meaningful questions that are forever beyond the reach of science... But if science cannot answer some ultimate question, what makes anybody think that religion can?

Comment: Dawkins doesn't think much of Gould's NOMA ideas – accusing him of 'bending over backwards... to positively supine lengths' (in other words, a lot). Dawkins' argument is simply that science is our best bet for answering every question and if it can't do so, there's nothing much else that can...

Stephen Jay Gould: Rocks of Ages: Science and Religion in the fullness of life pp9–10

Richard Dawkins: The God delusion p80

How Can Someone Who Lives by the 'Religious Method' Also Accept a Scientific Approach to Life?

◆ *Revelation of God's nature:* Many Christians accept that the revelation of God in history has to be understood in light of the time and place in which it was carried out. Just as human thinking has developed over time, so too has God's method of revealing himself. Ancient cultures had particular ways of understanding the divine, and God – if you like – matched that understanding by revealing himself in the most meaningful ways for those people then. Modern humans might think some of it was a bit 'unsophisticated', but it was right for the time and place.

For example, if Jesus was God as Christians believe, then he had access to all the knowledge and understanding which God has. This would mean that he would know about things which those humans around him would have known nothing of. Had he just blurted out all that knowledge, then those around him might have been either very confused by it, terrified by it, or might just have given up on him because such actions might lead them to wonder about his sanity.

So, God did what meant something to the people of the time – he didn't force their development by revealing more than they could handle. So, is it 'unscientific' to believe in the ways God revealed himself in the past? Do the obvious differences between how he revealed himself then and now make this historical stuff questionable? For Christians the answer is no – so you can be a scientist and accept that God revealed himself through history.

◆ *Revelation of God through Scripture*: Put simply, the Bible isn't a straightforward science textbook. It has other purposes. Some Christians will regard the Bible as containing scientific truths – even if those are not explained as we understand science now (see previous point). Other Christians simply argue that the Bible is a book which **guides** you in your life through relating your current circumstances to the writings within it. It isn't meant to explain how God created the Universe in scientific terms or explain scientific principles. So, when you try to answer scientific questions, you can use scientific method, when you are trying to answer questions of another nature you could use scriptures. So, you can be a scientist and accept that scripture is a way God has chosen to reveal himself.

◆ *Special revelation*: You can be a scientist and still believe in **miracles.** If you believe that God is all-powerful, then you would accept that God might choose to suspend the **laws of physics** for some reason. In this case, you don't need to understand it or be able to explain it scientifically, you simply accept it. The same applies to visions and dreams and God's 'appearances' and so on. This is one of the key points throughout this relationship which is as follows:

Science is about **facts** and religion is about **faith**. When you have faith you can accept what seem to be unacceptable facts. You can also interpret these facts as having some other kind of **symbolic** meaning which means that they won't trouble you for a scientific explanation. Some religious people have done precisely this by claiming for example that the 'miracles' of Jesus were symbolic, not literal. For example that he did not feed five thousand by actually miraculously creating more food, but that the boy's example in being willing to share what he had with others made the rest so impressed with his generosity that they produced their own food which they'd been keeping hidden up until then. So it was a 'miracle' of sorts, just not a supernatural one. Therefore you can be a scientist and accept miracles because those miracles can be reinterpreted or you can simply suspend your scientific approach to allow for the actions of an all-powerful God.

◆ *Revelation through the Church*: Now this is a tricky one because often the Church has taught things which are in direct opposition to the findings of science. So there are two possibilities. As a Christian, you might simply view the Church as a **human institution**, not one which has any special message from God. So, when it goes against scientific findings, it is simply humans getting it wrong. Another approach would be to accept that the Church is an institution which God does guide, but that his guidance, like all other kinds, does not mean turning his followers into robots by making them say what he wants them to. He may speak to the Church, but the Church might not get the message right at the time and have to review its position later (as it has done over Galileo and much more recently, Darwin). You might also take the view that God continues to guide the Church, but in matters related to 'religious' questions as opposed to entirely 'scientific' ones. This is similar to Gould's ideas about NOMA. So as a scientist you could accept that God reveals himself through the Church, but only when it is speaking about things which are 'religious' matters.

◆ *Revelation through religious experience*: As a scientist, you could argue that 'religious experience' is outside the scope of scientific testing because it relates to 'spiritual' matters – and science can't investigate spiritual things. This means that a scientist could have a religious experience – just not then explain what happened in scientific ways. This again refers to the idea of NOMA.

◆ *Revelation through order and design*: Although explaining the world around you can be achieved through science, perhaps that can only be done 'up to a point'. For example, although you can explain the structure and function of a flower, scientifically that doesn't entirely explain your sense that it is something beautiful. Now, you can argue that the perception of 'beauty' is just a particular set of neurons in your brain, firing in a particular order and so beauty is explainable scientifically – but for some people this just doesn't go far enough. They would argue that there is a sense in which humans appreciate the Universe around them in a '**spiritual**' way. This 'spiritual' dimension is outside of the scope of scientific enquiry – so you can accept that God has revealed himself through order and design in nature in a spiritual sense while accepting that science explains this order and design in a non-spiritual sense. You can therefore look at the Universe around you as something which points towards the existence of a God while also believing that you can understand it and (to an extent) control it through the appliance of science.

Summary

◆ Believing in God and believing in the methods and findings of science do not need to be **contradictions** as they are just **different** ways of understanding (non-overlapping magisteria).

◆ Belief in God involves **faith** as opposed to scientific **evidence** (perhaps even in the face of scientific evidence).

◆ Religion does not need to be **tested**, just **accepted**. This is not just 'blind faith', (though there is a place for that) but faith which is supported by reasonable argument and the teachings of the faith you follow however they have been received.

◆ Religious people believe that 'religious method' helps them to understand and answer 'religious questions'. Scientific method helps them to understand 'scientific questions', therefore there's no tension between the two.

How Can Someone Who Lives by the Scientific Method Also Accept a Religious Approach to Life?

◆ *Inductive reasoning*: Observation, hypothesis, experiment and verification/ falsification are all methods of researching scientific questions about things which can be observed and measured. But science is just that, a methodical approach to certain tasks. Life would become pretty odd if we started to approach everything using scientific method. In life, there are likely to be some things we just don't investigate scientifically – imagine someone applying scientific method to the question of whether or not someone else loves them. Religious matters are just the kinds of things which aren't 'open' to scientific enquiry because they deal with issues **outwith scientific expertise**. Also, science just doesn't have the tools for the job – there is no experimental procedure for measuring 'Godness', no piece of apparatus for discovering the whereabouts in a body of a soul and so on. So even if science could formulate the right questions (which perhaps it can't), it does not have the **equipment** to carry out any research which might follow. So, it is quite clear that scientific method has its **limitations** when asked to investigate 'spiritual things'. This isn't a weakness, just the way things are. No point in beating yourself up about them, just accept that science does what science does and religion does what religion does – no need to abandon either.

- *Scientific assumptions*: Some scientists might argue that scientific method often includes distinctly 'religious' ways of doing things. Many scientists have held onto a theory even when all the evidence has gone against them because they 'believe' that their theory is right. Others also 'believe' that their theory will be supported once the necessary techniques or apparatus become available to test their theory. But, up until that point their hypothesis looks a bit like a belief. Now, some would argue that they are not the same kind of 'beliefs' as exist in religion at all. Maybe so, maybe not – but many scientists can also accept religion because they feel that the assumptions of science are not very different to some of the assumptions of religion.

- *Verifying and falsifying:* Some scientists accept therefore that some things might never be verified or falsified using scientific means. This leaves the door open for them to accept a religious explanation.

- *Scientific models:* As you know, science uses models to describe things which are otherwise difficult to grasp. Some scientists argue that religious belief is no different. Their belief in a God is backed up (for them) by a particular model, or idea – and just as scientific models are only shadows of the real thing – so too are religious 'models' shadows of the real thing (which again, are outside of the scope of scientific enquiry).

- *Scientific objectivity*: Some scientists argue that science is, by its very nature, not as **objective** as it likes to think it is. Every interpretation of an observation, every choice of research method, or sample, or piece of apparatus or tool of statistical analysis involves subjectivity. This subjectivity maybe gets right in the way of discovering the 'truth'. Religious life is a subjectively interpreted thing – and if science can accept such subjectivity in scientific method, why criticise in relation to religion.

◆ *Evidence*: First of all, scientific evidence is often quite superficial, or not entirely there yet. It has to be interpreted and it is sometimes not very **conclusive**. This means that it can be **accepted provisionally** or **rejected provisionally**. Secondly, some scientists argue that they can be religious people too because... religion has its own 'evidence'. Religious people believe that there is evidence of God's revelation through all of the 'religious methods' you have examined. Although this may not be the same as hard scientific evidence it is, nevertheless, evidence. As evidence it might be quite enough upon which to base your life – thank you very much.

Talk Point 19

Is it possible to be a religious scientist?

Summary

◆ Science is a particular process and religion is something different... you can therefore accept the teachings and methods of both.

◆ Some religious things are not open to scientific investigation therefore you can accept them or not by faith alone.

◆ There may be evidence for religious claims if you are prepared to accept its validity. It does not necessarily need to count against scientific explanations – even of the same thing.

Source 21

Science and Religion, Not So Different?

No progress will be made in the debate about religious belief unless participants are prepared to recognise that the issue of truth is as important to religion as it is to science. Dawkins invokes Bertrand Russell's parable of the teapot irrationally claimed to be in unobserved orbit in the solar system. Of course there are no grounds for belief in this piece of celestial crockery, but there are grounds offered for religious belief, though admittedly different people evaluate their persuasiveness differently. Religion does not have access to absolute proof of its beliefs but, on careful analysis, nor does science. In all realms of human inquiry, the interlacing of experience and interpretation introduces a degree of precariousness into the argument. Yet this does not mean that we cannot attain beliefs sufficiently well motivated to be the basis for rational commitment. →

Comment: Polkinghorne was formerly Professor of Mathematical Physics at Cambridge University. Here he argues that science and religion are both concerned with searching for the truth and that both require interpretation and analysis. Just because religion needs interpretation doesn't make it wrong.

John Polkinghorne, http://entertainment.timesonline.co.uk/tol/ arts_and_entertainment /the_tls/article2778493.ece

Simple Section Summary

◆ The concept of non-overlapping magisteria (NOMA) suggests that religions and science deal with different things.

◆ As long as both stick to what they are best at and don't try to answer the questions of the other area there should be no disagreements.

◆ Religion and science can therefore live happily side by side.

◆ Religious people can also accept scientific method because it is about the material world and religion is about the spiritual world.

◆ Because religion is a faith it means that not all the ends have to be 'tied up'.

◆ For example, a religious person could accept contradictions in the Bible or breaking the laws of physics in miracles.

◆ This is possible by applying faith or accepting a symbolic, not literal meaning for something.

◆ Spiritual things might be outside the scope of scientific enquiry and only answerable in religious ways.

◆ Scientists too can accept religious belief while practising science.

◆ This is also because they can separate out the two things treating one as material and the other as spiritual.

◆ The inconclusive and provisional nature of scientific method leaves 'room' for religious belief.

◆ Perhaps science and religion answer different questions or perhaps the same questions in different ways.

◆ This means that they don't have to be opposites but complementary.

Activities

Knowledge, Understanding, Analysis and Evaluation

1 The two guests on *Ivory Towers* weren't very grown-up during their discussion. Why might scientists and religious people feel very strongly about their own 'side' during discussions?

2 What is monotheism?

3 What explanations might there be for the 'survival' of science during the dark ages?

4 Why did many religious people become interested in the development of science in the Mediaeval and enlightenment periods?

5 Why did science often come into conflict with the Church?

6 Why was Darwin's theory of evolution such a challenge to the Church?

7 Why might many people find the issues involved in the science and religion debate difficult to grasp?

8 According to an opponent of religion, where might life's 'meaning' come from?

9 According to a religious person, where might life's 'meaning' come from?

10 What point was Pope John Paul making in the quote on page 58?

11 Why might someone argue that science comes from the devil? What 'evidence' might they base this view upon?

12 What evidence is there that religious people (including literalists) accept some of the benefits of science?

13 What explanation might a religious literalist give for occasions where science seems to say the opposite to the Bible?

14 Explain the importance of faith for the religious literalist.

15 How might a religious literalist question scientific observation and hypotheses?

16 According to religious literalists, science can be subjective – what do they mean by this and why is it a criticism? Do you think it is a valid criticism?

17 Do you agree that there are some things (e.g. spiritual issues) which science cannot investigate?

18 Describe two criticisms of religious literalism which a scientific materialist such as EO Wilson might make.

19 Explain one argument a scientific materialist would give to support the validity of scientific method.

20 'Assumptions' are used as a criticism of science by religious literalists. How do scientific materialists respond?

21 Explain two arguments a scientific materialist might use in criticising religious method.

22 What is meant by NOMA?

23 Explain how a religious person could accept that the Bible is true but also accept some of the findings of science.

24 Could a scientific materialist accept that a religious experience was real? Explain your answer.

25 Why, for a scientific materialist, might a plant be evidence that there is no God?

Active Learning

1 Create a timeline for your class about the landmarks in the history of the science/religion debate.

2 Write the script for and act out your own edition of *Ivory Towers*, but this time, make sure that the religious person and the scientific materialist have a reasonable discussion.

3 Create a graffiti board in your classroom with three sections: 'Why religion is right'; 'Why science is right' and 'Why religion and science are both right'. Include quotes and comments on your board and illustrate each section appropriately.

4 Have a balloon debate in your class (three people in a balloon – vote them off one by one according to their argument). Each person should take one of the positions covered on your graffiti board and argue their case.

5 Miracles in the Bible are often a source of disagreement between religious literalists and scientific materialists. Write a speech in defence of miracles from a religious literalist point of view, a criticism of miracles from a scientific materialist point of view and a speech which suggests that religion and science can actually agree over miracles.

6 Use the internet to find out more about the views of: EO Wilson, William A Dembski, Richard Dawkins and Duane T Gish (you'll meet him in the next section…). Make you own fact sheets about each one including biographical information and information about their views.

7 Discuss and come up with a list of things which your class thinks science cannot investigate using scientific method.

8 In the USA's state schools there is no teaching about religion allowed. Investigate the reasons for this and write your own view about it based on what you have learned (this'll help for the next section too…).

9 Create artwork which shows both the 'glories of science' and the 'glories of religion' (you might like to talk through their less desirable features too).

Unit Assessment Question

Higher:
'You can be both a scientist and a Christian.' Do you agree? Give reasons for your answer. **AE6**

Intermediate 2:
'Science explains how and the Bible explains why.' Why might some Christians agree with this statement? **AE6**

Sample Exam Question

Higher:
'Scientific method is a more reliable way to help us understand the world around us than religious belief.' Do you agree? Give reasons for your answer. **AE6**

Intermediate 2:
Are religion and science opposites? Give two reasons for your answer. **AE4**

Homework

Carry out some internet research in preparation for the next section. Other than their 'methods' what kinds of things do science and Christianity have disagreements about? Prepare a short talk for your class on your findings.

Personal Reflection

Is the way you understand the world closer to that of a religious literalist or a scientific materialist? How does your view affect how you live your life?

CHAPTER 5

What is the Origin of the Universe: Created by God?

There once was a being named God
who thought it all really quite odd
that he lived all alone in the void
so a fantastic scheme he deployed:
'I'll make a Universe' thought he,
'with all sorts of life, now, let's see,
I'll fill up this cold empty space
with life forms in every place.'

Day One, 'Now let there be light!
That'll stop folks from getting a fright.'
All God had to do was to say (perhaps to angels),
'Let's separate out night from day.'
Then the waters and land they were parted
and work on the good Earth was started
and God said, 'It's my solemn intent
to create a great big firmament.'

And all this was done on Day Two
leaving God with still much to do.
Then God made the land and the seas
and added some very nice trees
including some very strange weeds
and other weird plants yielding seeds.
'Not a bad job as you'll see
and I've only just finished Day Three!'

'This is actually jolly fine fun'
said God as he fashioned the sun.
'A moon too to make the night bright
now there's a quite magical sight.
Some bright stars, though further away,
quite a feat and it's just the Fourth Day.'
Day Five now and still empty sky,
so God made some things that could fly.

In the waters as yet was no form,
so God made some creatures to swarm
like jellyfish, sharks and whales
and others with strange-looking tails.
Day Six was a busy one too
where God made a whole Earth-sized zoo
there were cattle and beasties and bugs
creepy-crawlies and slimy black slugs.
'Now what shall I finish it with?

A snork or a crudge or a fith?
No, I think I'll do what I can
with the dust and form woman and man.
Well, I think that I've now done my best,
on Day Seven I'm having a rest.'
God saw that it was good
and he hoped that it would stay that way...

Compare this with the original Genesis creation story in the Bible!

Talk Point

20

Do people still believe in the creation story in Genesis? What challenges might modern science present to these beliefs?

The Christian Creation Story

Source 22

Creation and Science: One View

It is a pity that the term 'Creation Science' was ever invented. Creation is not a branch of science, and never can be. Creation is a matter of faith, one of the fundamental beliefs of Christianity.

Comment: Dr Alan Hayward is a physicist and a 'Bible-believing Christian'. He argues that belief in God's creation is a matter of faith, not one of science and he questions Christians who have, in his opinion, confused religious matters such as creation with scientific ones.

Alan Hayward: Creation and Evolution – the Facts and the Fallacies: Triangle Publishing 1985, p206

The first book of the Old Testament is called **Genesis.** This word means something like 'how things came to be'. This Jewish text, accepted by Christians and Muslims alike, describes how the Universe began – or actually, to be more precise, it focuses on things from a particularly Earth-centred and human-centred viewpoint. Those who accept the belief that God created the Universe don't really get into the issue of the creation of other worlds (or any life on them). Perhaps, if this story is true, there are other similar stories all across the Universe describing how God created that particular planet and all its life forms (maybe he decided that 'snorks' or 'crudges' or 'friths' would be the dominant life forms on some other planetary system). However, that's not our concern here. Within Christianity, this story, found at the very beginning of the Bible in Genesis Chapter 1, describes how God created the Universe and goes into more detail about our Earth and all the life on it.

Where Did This Story Come From?

One of the first questions some people ask about this story is 'how does anyone know about it?' Obviously, if it is true, then the only person around at the time was God himself. So, how did the story come to be written down and who filled in all the details? Go back and have a look at the first section on religious method and just remind yourself about the different ways in which Christians understand the Bible. Here are some possibilities which cover both those Christians who take the story literally and those who don't:

◆ *Divine revelation*: The writers of the Bible were **inspired** by God. This means that God spoke through them. In a way, he 'possessed' them while they were writing the Bible and so what they wrote comes direct from him. God might also have guided them in what to write in a less dramatic way but it all amounts to the same thing. The story has come directly from God through the human writers of the Bible. If this is so, then we can assume that this is what happened – why would God have them write it down if it were wrong? Some Christians therefore think that the story is exactly what happened whereas others, while agreeing that it has come from God, think it is a story to explain something otherwise too complicated to understand.

◆ *Oral tradition*: The story ends with the creation of mankind. In the early Genesis stories, God speaks directly to his newly-formed creation and so presumably told them something about the creation story. This was passed down by word of mouth from Adam and Eve directly to their descendants and so on down the ages. Once writing was developed, the story was written down so that it could be preserved and eventually, as you would expect, found its way into the Bible. Some Christians will think that this oral tradition means that the story we have is unchanged from the story told by God to Adam and Eve; others might argue that it has all become a little more poetic and a little less accurate as it has been passed down throughout the ages.

◆ *A myth based on the observable Universe:* For some Christians, the Genesis creation story is a **myth**. This doesn't mean that it's untrue, just that it's a kind of writing where an attempt is made to explain the unexplainable. There is some truth in it, but that truth is hard to pinpoint, so the general meaning of the story (that God did it all) becomes more important than the specific details which you don't need to take too literally. As early humans looked around at their Universe, they came to the conclusion that something must have made it because it was all too vast and amazing to have been made by anything human. They therefore came up with explanations about what must have happened based on what they could see. The story therefore was not passed on by God, but just represents a way of explaining how it must have been based on what you see around you. Therefore you don't have to believe any part of the creation story, but – and it's an important but – you can still believe that God created the Universe...

The Creation Story in Genesis 1: A Literal Interpretation

Christian Literalists believe that the creation story in Genesis Chapter 1 is absolutely true in every respect. They believe that the Bible is **God's word** and so we must accept everything written in it. We might well find some of the writing in it hard to understand and even some of it a little hard to accept, but we should do so anyway. That, after all, is what faith is about. Humans are not God after all and we can't see into the mind of God (we couldn't cope with it if we could) – so what we have to do is simply trust and believe. Besides which, if we start arguing that some parts of the Bible are literally true and others are not, how do we

decide which is which? We'd really get ourselves into an awful mess by doing this and so the best approach is simply to accept that the Bible has come from God and so every word is absolute truth. We don't need to understand it; we just need to accept it. So if the Bible says that God created the Universe in six days then that's what happened. It is also important to remember that Christians believe that one of the characteristics of God is that he is **omnipotent.** This means **all-powerful** – in other words he can do anything. So, he can not only create the Universe in six days, he can also do it exactly as Genesis says he did.

One further point: Christian Literalists might well point out that Genesis 1 is not written as part of a science textbook. For example, the creation of light itself is summed up as follows: *'And God said, 'Let there be light!' and there was light'* (Genesis 1:3). This is the barest amount of detail about the creation of something about which scientists today still can't agree – is it a wave/force or a particle (leading to the wave-particle duality theory)? So, why would God have felt any need to include what would be unbelievably complex maths and physics at the start of the Bible? In fact, had God described exactly how he created light, would we ever have understood it anyway? Christian literalists argue quite simply that God is God and we're not. If it says that's how the Universe was created in his word then that's how it was.

So, the Christian Literalist position summarised is:

◆ If it's in the Bible it's true.

◆ God can do anything and so the story is as it's written.

◆ The Bible is a book of faith, not of science.

◆ The biblical creation story does all that it needs to – pointing to God as the creator of everything.

Creationists

Creationists are Christians who believe in the **literal truth** of the biblical creation story. They argue that because the Bible is the inspired word of God, its teachings are God's truth. Therefore, the Bible story of the creation is also true – exactly as it happened. Creationists argue that any scientific evidence which goes against the Bible's teachings is simply wrong. You'll look at their arguments in more detail later...

Source 23

Days Means Days

I do not accept the... idea that the six days were millions of years long because the only reason for accepting this is to make the Bible agree with evolution

Comment: This Creationist view argues that we should not try to re-interpret things in the Bible to fit with scientific findings. If the Bible says it's a day, then it's a day.

Professor EH Andrews, From Nothing to Nature (Evangelical Press, Welwyn 1978) p63

Strengths and Limitations of Christian Literalism

Strengths	Limitations
• Requires faith alone – no need to understand complicated scientific theories or ideas	• Does not take into account scientific evidence which contradicts biblical teachings
• Means that the Bible can be accepted as an authoritative source without having to spend too much time interpreting and analysing it – a fairly simple approach to life	• Is too simplistic and therefore is a rejection of the intelligence which even a Christian literalist thinks is a gift from God. Ignores the possibility that the Bible is there as a general guide rather than as something which is to be taken completely at face value
	• If the Bible is taken at face value then that means that many other teachings in it might have to be accepted too – some which might not seem all that desirable in today's world

The Creation Story in Genesis 1: A Symbolic Interpretation

Other Christians might argue that the creation story is true but in a **symbolic** way. For example, the 'days' of creation might be understood as geological time-periods, or single events separated by long periods of time or some other understanding of the meaning of the word 'day'. What it might not mean is a 24-hour period of time. Literalists are wary of interpretations like this because it seems as if it's an example of Christians trying to **accommodate** the findings of science.

However, many Christians do understand the creation story symbolically – as something which points to the truth through **imagery**, **allegory** and **metaphor** but which is not true in the absolute factual sense. For this kind of Christian, the 'days' of creation do not need to be 24-hour periods. They might also point to the lack of hard scientific detail in the creation story – had it been meant to be factually true then perhaps God might have included more scientific detail in it. No, according to such Christians, the purpose of the story is to convey the simple message that God created the Universe. Exactly *how* he did so is not important. What is important is *that* he did so.

Symbolic interpretations of the creation story have the advantage that they mean Christians do not have to respond to what are claimed to be scientifically demonstrated truths – such as the age of the Earth or the extinction of species. A literal interpretation might mean that you have to accept that God created life then as it is now and so the extinction of the dinosaurs will present you with some problems. However, if you argue that the story in Genesis 1 is symbolic then you do not have that difficulty, or many others (*who did Adam and Eve's son have children by?* and so on…)

Understanding the creation story symbolically, in summary:

◆ If it's in the Bible it can be true, but it can be symbolically expressed rather than factually.

◆ God can do anything, but the story describes that in 'pictures' we can understand.

◆ The Bible is a book of faith, but we still need to match the findings of science with the claims of religion in an intelligent way – symbolically interpreting the creation story allows us to do that.

◆ The biblical creation story points to God as the creator – but does so through a story which has to be interpreted as symbolism and myth.

Talk Point

Is a symbolic interpretation of the creation story just a cop-out?

Source 24

Symbolically Interpreting the Bible

The Bible tells us what happens when we take the life of faith seriously. In many ways it is a very human piece of work, full of the prejudices, exaggerations and misjudgements which belong to every human work. But that is by no means the whole story. One of the most remarkable features of the Bible is that the more one recognises that the people who wrote it were ordinary human beings, the more one becomes aware of the extraordinary insights and experiences which they were trying to grapple with.

Comment: Habgood was a Christian who argues that we have to read the Bible intelligently and not simply take everything at face value. This means that we have to approach the Bible critically and try to make sense of what its writers were trying to communicate rather than simply accept it as written. The writers lived in a different world which modern understanding of the Bible has to take into account.

John Habgood: Religion & Science: Mills & Boon 1964 p79

Strengths and Limitations of Symbolically Interpreting the Scriptures

Strengths	Limitations
• Allows you to explain away things in the Bible which would be ridiculous if they were interpreted literally	• You need to be sure which things are meant to be understood symbolically and which are not – there may be a danger of 'picking' and choosing' what you believe and so not living a life of faith at all – instead 'making God in your own image'
• Is the correct use of god-given intelligence in analysing and interpreting a complex source	• If you ignore some parts of the Bible and not others there is a danger that you will eventually reject it all and so lose your faith entirely
• Means that you are part of the way to accepting at least some of the findings of science and so less likely to reach a point where your faith and science simply disagree	• If you start to doubt the Bible then you might be swayed by the power of the scientific findings into complete religious disbelief

Simple Section Summary

◆ Christians believe that the Universe was created by God and the Bible describes this

◆ The Bible creation story may have been divinely inspired by God

◆ The story may have been passed down through the ages

◆ The story may only have symbolic meaning

◆ Christian literalists believe that the Universe was created by God exactly as the Bible describes it

◆ Creationists believe that the Bible story of creation is literally true

◆ Some Christians believe that the Bible creation story is a myth – including some truth but also metaphor and allegory as well as symbolic meaning

Who Made God: Aquinas's Cosmological (First Cause) Argument

No matter whether the Christian response to the creation story treats it as literally true or symbolic, one important issue is raised. If God existed before the creation of the Universe, where and when did he exist and also – importantly – what are his origins? Christians of all sorts answer that God is an **uncreated** being. He is without beginning and without end and that the question of God's origins is therefore a non-starter. One of the first and most well known arguments in this respect is the argument of Thomas Aquinas (1224–1274). Aquinas's **cosmological argument** goes like this:

◆ Everything which exists is **caused** (or 'moved' to use Aquinas's own words) to exist by something else.

◆ Therefore everything in the Universe must have been caused to exist by something coming before it.

◆ There must therefore have been a **first cause** to all of this because it is not logical that it could go on backwards into infinity.

◆ At the beginning there must have been something which itself was **uncaused** to set in motion the chain of all following causes.

◆ The only being that can, by definition, be uncaused is God.

◆ Therefore God must be the first cause.

◆ Therefore God exists.

Aquinas argued that **contingent** beings require a cause. Because this cannot go back in time forever there must exist a **necessary** being which was uncaused. That would be God. Further to this, most Christians argue that God created the Universe out of nothing (**ex nihilo**) he didn't use already existing material – because there wasn't any – he made it from what did not exist (after bringing it into existence).

Accepting the First Cause Argument

◆ It is a matter of faith (though for Aquinas it was principally a matter of reason. God exists and the definition of God is that he is the uncreated creator. Therefore the First Cause argument must be true.

◆ Accepting the argument does away with the (illogical) need to accept that cause and caused go back in time **infinitely.**

◆ The argument fits with what most Christians already believe about God as the initial creator of all things and so all it does is give a philosophical form to a belief which Christians 'feel' is right.

◆ To say that God is uncaused even though everything needs a cause is not a contradiction because God is a special case.

◆ For some Christians, the flaws in the cosmological argument are clear. However, they turn to other, in their opinion more convincing, arguments for the existence of God such as the argument from religious experience and so on.

Talk Point

Before looking at the arguments against the First Cause argument below, talk through in class what the possible flaws in this argument might be.

Rejecting the First Cause Argument

◆ You cannot logically say that everything needs a cause and then say immediately afterwards that God doesn't. If everything needs a cause so does God. If however, God does not need a cause, then why does the Universe? It is just as likely that it is 'uncaused' as that God is.

◆ Introducing the idea of an uncaused God just makes your problem worse. In using the idea of God as the cause of all causes, you just create the need for an even bigger, more powerful and complex being who could cause God (and so on, backwards forever).

◆ Even if you argue successfully that all causes require a cause and that cause is a divine being, you have not absolutely proved that this being is what Christians call God. Perhaps there was a committee of Gods or perhaps... That God wasn't at all anything like the God of Christianity.

◆ Maybe the first cause was the Christian God. But him being the first cause does not prove that he's still around. Perhaps the act of creation was so exhausting that he 'died'. Or perhaps he created it all and then decided to have nothing more to do with it afterwards.

◆ **Quantum physics** presents the First Cause argument with some big problems. It suggests that some things in the quantum Universe do seem to spontaneously appear and disappear....without any cause. If this is so, then science has solid evidence that the statement 'all things require a cause' is wrong. This would completely do away with the need for any uncaused first cause.

Source 25

The Cosmological Argument: For and Against

All three of [Thomas Aquinas's proofs for the existence of God] rely upon regress and invoke God to terminate it. They make the entirely unwarranted assumption that God himself is immune to the regress. Even if we allow the dubious luxury of arbitrarily conjuring up a terminator to an infinite regress and giving it a name, simply because we need one, there is absolutely no reason to endow that terminator with any of the properties normally ascribed to God...

Comment: Dawkins reflects the argument that wanting to identify the starting off point of all causes as God isn't any more likely than that it was something else – perhaps nothing like God.

Richard Dawkins: The God Delusion p101

All in all then, Christians argue that God created the Universe. The biblical creation story points to this either as a factual account or a symbolic version. Either way it makes it clear that God caused it all. Aquinas's argument tries to take this further by suggesting that in addition to the teachings of the Bible, there are reasonable philosophical grounds for believing in God as the creator of the Universe. However, Aquinas wrote long before the rise of modern science and those Christians who accept the creation story of the Bible, whether literally or symbolically, have something which they must now take into account in the form of the Big Bang Theory.

Strengths and Limitations of Religious Explanations for the Origin of the Universe

Strengths	Limitations
• Based on 'evidence' from the creator himself	• Based on belief only with no scientific support
• Gives a simple and understandable account of the origin of the Universe	• Uses biblical texts and philosophical arguments which are all open to a variety of interpretations – and these interpretations are based only on different beliefs about them
• Suggest meaning and purpose for human life and suggests the existence of a creator who is there for us and cares about our existence	

Simple Section Summary

◆ The cosmological argument came from Thomas Aquinas.
◆ This states that everything requires a cause.
◆ Therefore there must have been a first cause.
◆ Therefore that must have been God.
◆ God did not need a cause according to Christians but scientific materialists argue that if everything needs a cause, so too must God. If not, perhaps the Universe needs no cause.
◆ Christians can accept the cosmological argument through faith while scientific materialists reject it as illogical and lacking evidence.
◆ For example, a scientific materialist might argue that even if the argument is correct it does not need to lead to belief in the God of Christianity.

Activities

Knowledge, Understanding, Analysis and Evaluation

1 What does Alan Hayward say about 'Creation Science'? Do you agree?

2 What problems does the existence of the creation story in Genesis present for us?

3 What possible ways are there for the creation story in Genesis to have ended up in the Bible we have today?

4 What is a Creationist?

5 What is meant by a 'myth'?

6 What would a Christian Literalist believe about the Genesis creation story?

7 What might the idea of God being 'omnipotent' have to do with the Genesis creation story?

8 Why might some Christians (like EH Andrews) be concerned about other Christians who try to explain that the 'days' in the Genesis story might mean something other than 24 hour periods?

9 What is meant by understanding the Genesis creation story symbolically?

10 What view does John Habgood have about understanding the Bible?

11 In your own words, explain Aquinas's Cosmological Argument.

12 What is the biggest question linked to the Cosmological Argument? What are your class's views on this?

13 Explain how someone can accept the Cosmological Argument.

14 In your opinion, is there a need for a first cause? Does an uncaused cause make any more sense?

15 What is meant by creation 'ex nihilo'?

16 Explain why someone might reject the Cosmological Argument.

17 How might the theories of quantum physics harm the Cosmological Argument?

Active Learning

1 To prepare you for future study, do an internet search on 'Creation Science' and 'Intelligent Design'. Present your findings to your class.

2 Find out about other creation myths. How many are similar to the Bible's creation story? How many are very different? Make a display of your findings.

3 Design an information leaflet for Christians based on a literal understanding of the creation story. You could do this as a FAQ sheet.

4 Have a class debate: 'Interpreting the Bible creation story symbolically shows a lack of faith'.

5 Investigate the life and teachings of Thomas Aquinas. You could then design an illustrated magazine-type article about his life and work.

6 Write a dialogue in the style of Rab and Donnie (or Robyn and Donna if you like) covering views about Aquinas's Cosmological Argument.

7 Find out more about quantum physics… Does it do away with the need for a first cause?

Unit Assessment Question

Higher:
'The cosmological argument fails to support the existence of God.' How might a Christian respond to this statement?
KU8

Intermediate 2:
What does it mean to say that some Christians understand the creation story symbolically?
KU4

Sample Exam Question

Higher:
'To be a Christian you must accept the truth of the creation story in Genesis 1.' Would a Christian agree? Give reasons for your answer.
AE6

Intermediate 2:
Explain how a Christian might argue that the creation story in Genesis 1 should be accepted as literally true.
AE4

Homework

Write a poem (in the form of the stimulus at the start of this section) to explain Aquinas's Cosmological Argument.

Personal Reflection

Do you think there must have been a first cause? Does it make a difference whether you believe there was one or not?

CHAPTER 6

What is the Origin of the Universe: The Big Bang?

About fifteen billion years ago
something was about to blow.
A rather odd peculiarity
now widely known as a singularity.

Where did it come from?
No one knew.
But one thing's sure,
it quickly grew.

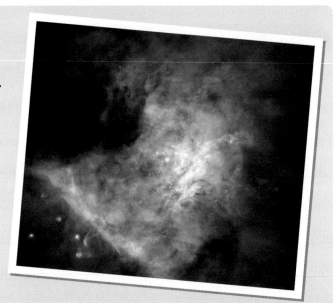

When did it happen? There's a
    trouble.
'When' doesn't work, says
    Dr Hubble.
Time itself began then too,
long before even Dr Who.

So if it happened – where?
And was there anyone there?
Nope, space began as well
and rapidly did swell.

Where is your proof, it all seems odd,
sounds like there's no need for God.
'That could be right,' one scientist said
'or perhaps he was there but quickly fled.'

I want evidence, give me some!
Or I'll take the huff and suck my thumb.
Evidence? Alright then, here's a bit
but you may feel a bit of a twit.

Matter in space is hurtling apart,
away from the force of the Bang at the start.
The evidence that you're demanding
is clear, the Universe is expanding.

And then there's all the elements
their abundance proof presents.
The Big Bang's matter we detect
is exactly what we should expect.

And finally to resolve frustration
there's just the right dose of radiation.
Now isn't it odd that this science–feast
was first proposed by a Catholic priest.

It's likely that most people in your class have heard of the
Big Bang, *but what do they know about it? Discuss in class
and identify the range of information and views which people
have about this theory (before you read what follows).*

Big Bang Theory

Yes, indeed, the Big Bang was first proposed by a Catholic priest named Georges Lemaitre in 1931 (he was though, a fully qualified scientist as well). He called this theory the 'hypothesis of the primeval atom'. Some scientists were worried about his theory because it suggested a beginning to the Universe which sounded a little… well … religious… Lemaitre's views however came to be accepted as part of the evidence supporting the idea that the Universe began in a Big Bang.

The theory comes under the general scientific heading of **cosmology** (or rather nowadays it is referred to as the standard model of cosmology as there have been modifications to it – but let's be grateful that the SQA hasn't noticed Superstring theory, M-Theory or Calabi-Yau space just yet). Anyway, the theory proposes that matter, time, energy and space all began in an instant as a super-hot, super-dense mixture of everything. Some scientists refer to this as a '**cosmic egg**'. This incredibly dense point became known as a **singularity** (sad really, as the idea of a cosmic egg is rather more poetic…).

This singularity, perhaps because of the mind-boggling physics involved in 'maintaining' it, suddenly exploded. Now the word 'explosion' isn't completely scientifically accurate, because an explosion suggests something and somewhere in which to explode out into, which wasn't the case with the Big Bang. So try to think of the 'explosion' of the Big Bang as looking at it from the inside rather than from the outside – and for the purposes of this book we'll use 'explosion'. The reason why this explosion took place is still unclear: if time and space came into existence at this point where did the 'laws' governing the whole process come from? However, it happened, and the force of the explosion brought into being time, space, energy and matter. The explosive matter, time and space now hurtled outwards, cooling and expanding as it went. So, let's be clear here: According to Big Bang Theory, at the moment of the Big Bang, three things came into being:

◆ **Matter**: Many of the elements which we know today such as Hydrogen and Helium all came into being as a result of that event. Some came later created in the stars, which of course came from matter which began at the Big Bang.

◆ **Space**: This is harder to get your head round because we usually think of space as nothing rather than something. However, according to physics, space is something, and according to Big Bang Theory, space also began at the start of the Universe (remember it is space itself that is expanding, not stuff expanding into space).

◆ **Time**: For some, this is the most difficult idea to grasp, because we think of time as an idea rather than as anything actually solid and concrete. However, again, time is considered by physicists to have physical properties and so it too began – even though our use of the word 'began' implies a time-period at a time when there was no time (no one said this was going to be easy). In fact, one of the alternative names for the Big Bang is '**time zero**' or **t=0**.

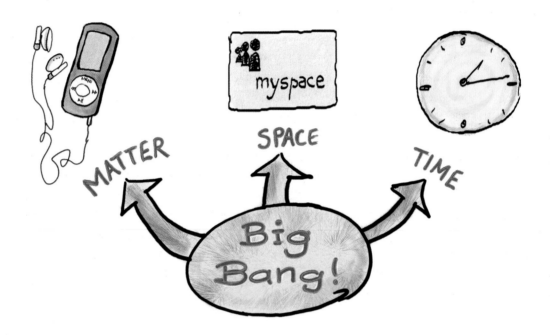

All of this means that one answer to the question of where and when the Big Bang happened is right now, wherever you are, because all the space and time in which you currently exist was compressed into those Big Bang **initial conditions** (!). You can add to this complex equation energy, though this is a little more confusing since to say that the **energy** of the Universe was 'created' at the moment of the Big Bang implies that the energy of the Big Bang came from nothing – going against one of the prime laws of physics – that something cannot come from nothing... But (and it's a very large but) something called **quantum physics** suggests that matter can actually come into being completely **spontaneously** – out of **nothing.** If this can happen, and it seems to be so, then it is just possible that the Universe did in fact just happen out of nowhere and nothing. However, it's an RMPS book, not a physics book, so let's leave it at that. Remember that religious views also have the Universe being created by God out of nothing (ex nihilo).

Following the initial Big Bang, **gravitational** forces of collapse and condensation caused the gases and elements produced at the moment of the Big Bang to clump together (the timescales vary from fractions of a second to hundreds of thousands of years...). As they did so, they formed energy reactions and stars began to form which in turn produced additional elements. Space darkened and clusters of stars formed galaxies. These new stars had massive gravitational pull and the free matter around them began to cluster together forming asteroids, comets and planets just like our own home - planet Earth. The force of the Big Bang is still with us today as galaxies and space-time expand outwards from the Big Bang singularity .Some scientists propose that this expansion will eventually come to a halt and, as matter cools further and condenses, it will eventually start to contract under gravitational force… right back to another singularity (sometimes referred to as a **Big Crunch**) and the whole process might begin all over again…and again…

Evidence for the Big Bang

The evidence for the Big Bang is, in some ways, **circumstantial**. The Big Bang is **inferred** from what we can observe and explain today and what therefore must have caused it is too. This 'working back' to what must have been is, according to science, more than mere guesswork – it is the logical application of observable reality to explain what was not (by definition) observed. The evidence for the Big Bang is an interesting example of how the scientific method sometimes works. Big Bang Theory is a collection of different findings and theories which were put together and added to the store of explanations about how the Universe might have begun. Some of the theories were based on demonstrated evidence, and others were based on assumptions which at the time could not be supported by the evidence (but later were) because the techniques for gathering the evidence were not yet available. Some of the evidence for the Big Bang is therefore observable and measurable (**empirical evidence**) and some is **theoretical**, awaiting the right techniques to turn it into empirical evidence.

The Expanding Universe

When you hear the siren of a fire-engine coming towards you and then moving away from you, you'll notice that the pitch of its siren changes from high to low (NEE NAW, nee naw, nee naw, nee naw) This is caused by the **Doppler Effect** where the sound waves of the siren are compressed and then stretched as the vehicle moves about you. A similar process happens with light. Edwin Hubble, an astronomer (and former lawyer who turned down the chance to be a professional boxer) at the Mount Wilson observatory in California, discovered that the light coming from distant galaxies was all shifted towards the red end of the light spectrum (light waves have distinctive patterns which can tell us lots of useful information about their source). Although the **cosmological red shift** isn't completely explained by the Doppler Effect, it points to the suggestion that cosmological red shift implies an expanding Universe. In 1927, Hubble found that this was the case, and so, this red shift must

mean that things in the Universe were moving apart (imagine it like dots on an inflating balloon moving apart from each other – remember though, it's space itself which is expanding).

Hubble therefore proposed that the Universe must in fact be expanding. Of course, if the Universe was expanding then it had to have expanded 'from' somewhere. Hubble measured this rate of expansion and then by running the events 'backwards', predicted that it must have expanded from a central point at some specific time in the Universe's past. This event became known as the Big Bang and the point as the singularity.

Ten years before Hubble's discovery, Albert Einstein might just have beaten him to it in the discovery of the Big Bang. Einstein proposed – though only theoretically – that the lifespan of the Universe is limited by the energy in it. To cut a long, and complicated, story short:

Source 26

Almost, But Not Quite

By Einstein's simplest formula, [the Universe] is due to expand to a maximum diameter of about 40,000 million light-years. Its total lifespan from its explosive genesis to its comprehensive doomsday is, by this reckoning, about 63,000 million years… If only Einstein's nerve had held, here would have been his master stroke. He would have predicted the recession of the galaxies that Edwin Hubble announced ten years later and, long before anyone else, he would have promulgated the Big Bang as the origin of the Universe. But in 1917 no one imagined that the Universe was anything like that.

Comment: Einstein argued that all systems in the Universe had a finite store of energy. Because the energy of the Universe is not infinite it could not have existed for all eternity. The logical conclusion of this is that it must have had some kind of beginning.

Nigel Calder: Einstein's Universe; Penguin 1979 p208

Einstein suggested that the Universe should eventually run out of **energy** and return to a kind of crash (recede). Lemaitre had also proposed the theoretical existence of a moment in space and time at which everything began. However, it was Hubble who actually demonstrated that the Universe was indeed expanding (and so would eventually probably recede).

This expansion implied two important things:

◆ Everything in the Universe appeared to be expanding away from a central 'point', so there must have been such a starting-off point and so for everything a 'beginning'.

◆ Einstein's theory of general relatively supported this view; because in the theory of general relativity he concluded that the whole Universe was changing in size and in time – not just 'sitting still'. However, Einstein felt that this couldn't be right and so he came up with something called the **cosmological constant** to explain it away. However, once Hubble came up with his evidence, Einstein had to abandon his cosmological constant and accept that the Universe was indeed expanding.

Hubble demonstrated what Einstein and Lemaitre had only theorised, and so Hubble's theory became the accepted origin of Big Bang theory.

Cosmic Background Radiation

The second piece of evidence for the Big Bang came in 1965. Two astronomers working in radio astronomy (as opposed to looking through optical telescopes), Arno Penzias and Robert Wilson, found that their reception had a kind of noisy fuzz associated with it (imagine that hiss you get when your TV is not tuned into a channel). This fuzz seemed to be coming from every point in the Universe and was measured as having a temperature of –270 degrees.

After some initial confusion, physicists agreed that this background fuzz was leftover 'heat' in the form of radiation. Think of a sparkler on bonfire night. You light it and it gets very hot. It also heats up whatever is around it (in that case, air molecules). The sparkler itself will take some time to cool down, but so too (if you could measure it) would the heated-up air around it. Now multiply the energy from this sparkler to the energy which must have been present at the Big Bang. The background 'heat' is still there and still cooling some fifteen billion years after the event (although the sparkler 'loses' heat to the surrounding air and the Universe cannot lose heat to something surrounding it as there isn't anything…). So, the initial Big Bang explosion had left behind a 'signature' in the form of remaining **microwave radiation** and this radiation can be both observed and measured today (referred to as **Cosmic background radiation**). All the observations point to a moment in the Universe's past where everything began in an instant.

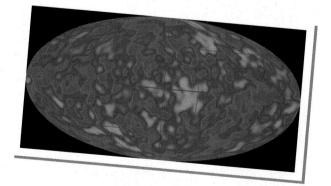

Relative Abundance of the Elements

Suppose you mix up a couple of eggs and some milk… you have an omelette or scrambled eggs. Next time you add some butter and flour – now you have pancakes. Next time you add some sugar and baking powder – now you've got a cake. Of course the cooking process for each of these is slightly different: bake your omelette mixture for 45 minutes and you'll probably have something you could play football with. Each mixture uses different ingredients and has to be treated in a different way. Now suppose that you had in front of you a cake, a pancake and an omelette. Using some scientific technique (perhaps like a mass spectrometer, though it's doubtful if anyone would waste their time doing such a thing) you could work out what the ingredients were and roughly how they were put together and cooked.

You can actually do something similar with the Big Bang. The Universe today contains the **elements**, the basic atomic and chemical building blocks for everything that exists. The amounts of these (their relative abundance) in the Universe today points very strongly towards a particular process of their 'creation' in the past – in fact, the evidence points to the Big Bang. For example, Hydrogen is the most abundant element in the Universe, about 90 per cent of the atoms in the Universe are Hydrogen atoms, but why is there so much Hydrogen? Again, without getting into the mathematical complexities, the proportion of Hydrogen in the Universe today is exactly what you would expect if the Universe had been started off by a Big Bang.

Talk Point   24

If the Big Bang theory is correct, what might this mean for religious beliefs?

Small Breathing Space

This is complex stuff and you're probably wondering how much detail is needed for an RMPS course. Obviously, the more detail you can include the better (but watch the balance of your answers). The markers are not Physics graduates (actually some of them probably are) and they want to know that you have a basic understanding of Big Bang Theory and so can relate it to religious belief. So here's a quick summary:

◆ The Big Bang was a big explosion which started off the Universe.

◆ Space, time, energy and matter began at this point.

◆ We have evidence for the Big Bang in:

　◆ the expanding Universe
　◆ background radiation levels
　◆ relative abundance of the elements.

◆ The Big Bang caused itself.

What Caused the Big Bang?

The evidence above is regarded by scientists as pretty conclusive support for the Big Bang theory. However, there remains the question of why the Big Bang ever happened in the first place. Did time and space 'have' to begin? Couldn't the singularity have remained exactly as it was for all eternity? Finally, and for us perhaps the most significant, why did this all have to lead to a Universe where someone like you could be sitting reading this book? (And is there life all over the Universe or – perhaps more strangely – is our microscopic little planet the only place where there are thinking beings…? And so on.) Some of these questions we'll examine later, but for the moment let's consider why the Big Bang happened – was it inevitable?

Source 27

What Caused the Big Bang?

Whenever I give a lecture on cosmology one question never fails to be asked: What caused the Big Bang? A few years ago I had no real answer. Today, I believe we know what caused the Big Bang… The explanation can be summarised as follows: with gravitational attraction the only cosmic force available, the Big Bang must simply be accepted as god-given, a event without a cause, an assumed initial condition.

Comment: Davies is a professor of Theoretical Physics. In his book he reminds us that had the Big Bang been any 'stronger' or 'weaker' the Universe (as we know it) would not exist at all. He argues that gravitational force somehow reached a critical point where the singularity 'had' to explode. In essence the Universe caused itself. The initial conditions which led to the Big Bang are still unexplained.

→

Davies follows up this argument in another book, 'The Mind of God' where he refers to work by Stephen Hawking. Hawking suggests that the Universe, because it was the beginning of time and space, needed no 'cause'. Davies proposes:

Is it therefore correct to say that the Universe has 'created itself'? The way I would rather express it is that the Universe of space-time and matter is internally consistent and self-contained. Its existence does not require anything outside of it; specifically no prime mover is needed.

Paul Davies: Superforce; Unwin 1985 p183&184

Paul Davies: The Mind of God; Penguin 1992 p83

In physics therefore, the Big Bang requires **no cause** other than the **laws of nature** (for example, the law of gravity). Still, this leads to a further question – did the laws of nature come into being at the moment of the Big Bang? If they did, then they could not have caused the Big Bang because they didn't exist before it. One current theory comes from James Hartle and Stephen Hawking which seems to cast doubt on the idea of the space-time singularity. However, if (and its one of the biggest 'ifs' in cosmology) the laws of nature existed before the Big Bang, how did they come to be? This search for the '**initial conditions**' of the Big Bang goes on today. For scientists, this remains the key to the complete understanding of Big Bang theory.

Source 28

A Theory of Everything?

Valiant attempts by physicists such as Hawking and James Hartle... have tried to bring the question of cosmological conditions within the umbrella of physical theory, but all such attempts remain inconclusive... our cosmological understanding is, at present, just too primitive to determine whether our candidate 'theory of everything' truly lives up to its name and determines its own cosmological initial conditions, thereby elevating them to the status of physical law. This is a prime question for future research.

Comment: Greene is Professor of physics and mathematics at Columbia University and Cornell University. His book outlines some of the latest developments in this complex field. However, he points out here that work remains to be done in finding the answers to questions about the initial causes of the Big Bang which remains, still, a mystery.

Brian Greene: The elegant Universe: Superstrings,
hidden dimensions and the quest for the ultimate theory: Vintage 2000 p366

Strengths and Limitations of the Big Bang Theory

Strengths	Limitations
• Strong scientific basis for the theories from a variety of fields of scientific enquiry.	• Based on much circumstantial evidence which is not as powerful as empirical evidence.
• Offers a rational inferential explanation for something which occurred by definition without anyone there to observe it.	• Is so complex that it is not a useful way for ordinary people to understand how the Universe began.
	• Perhaps does not offer any explanations as to the meaning and purpose of human life or our place in the Universe.

Simple Section Summary

◆ Scientific materialists believe that the Universe began with a Big Bang.

◆ In this, matter, time, energy and space were all created.

◆ The Big Bang does not need any creator – it 'created' itself.

◆ The evidence for the Big Bang is:
  – Expanding Universe – Universe is expanding implying an 'explosive' beginning.
  – Cosmic background radiation – amount of radioactive 'heat' present in the Universe suggests a Big Bang.
  – Relative abundance of the elements – the materials present in the Universe match up with what you'd expect if there had been a Big Bang.

◆ The search for the 'initial conditions' for the Big Bang (i.e. why did it happen at all) still continue today.

Activities

Knowledge, Understanding, Analysis and Evaluation

1 What did Georges Lemaitre propose and why might some scientists have been concerned about it?

2 What is a singularity?

3 Why might it be wrong to say that the singularity 'exploded'?

4 What came into being at the Big Bang?

5 How does quantum physics support the idea of the Big Bang?

6 Following the Big Bang how did stars and planets come into being?

7 What's the Big Crunch?

8 What does it mean to say that the evidence for the Big Bang is circumstantial?

9 What's the difference between empirical evidence and theory?

10 What did Edwin Hubble discover and how did this link to Big Bang Theory?

11 How did Einstein try to explain away his theory that the Universe must be expanding?

12 How does Cosmic Background Radiation support the Big Bang Theory?

13 How does the relative abundance of the elements support the Big Bang Theory?

14 Why does the question 'what caused the Big Bang?' still cause problems for science?

15 What is meant by the 'initial conditions' for the Big Bang?

16 In what way is some of the Big Bang Theory still 'a mystery'?

17 If the Big Bang Theory is true, would that harm religious belief?

18 Could a scientist believe in God and still accept the Big Bang Theory?

Active Learning

1 Design an information poster or PowerPoint presentation on the Big Bang Theory. Try to make this very complex material as simple as you can. Perhaps you could set yourself a target of trying to explain it to an S1 class…

2 Create short illustrated biographies of some of the scientists you have come across in this section, for example, Lemaitre, Einstein, Hawking, Hubble, Penzias & Wilson, etc.

3 Paint some dots on an un-inflated balloon. Now inflate it and watch space expand!

4 Find out about some of the properties of light and of gravity. Present your findings to your class.

5 Using the information you have gathered for tasks 1 and 2 in this section, write a short speech outlining the contribution of one scientist to the development of the Big Bang Theory.

6 Come up with two lists about the Big Bang – one of 'answered questions' and the other 'unanswered questions'. Or, if you like, come up with an ABC of the Big Bang – e.g. A is for atoms, all of which came into being at the moment of the Big Bang, B is for Big Bang etc.

Unit Assessment Question

Higher:
What do scientists understand by the Big Bang?   **KU6**

Intermediate 2:
Describe two pieces of supporting evidence for the Big Bang Theory.   **KU4**

Sample Exam Question

Higher:
The evidence for the Big Bang cannot be disputed: Do you agree?   **AE6**

Intermediate 2:
Can a Christian accept the Big Bang Theory? Give reasons for your answer.   **AE4**

Homework

Write the main points of the Big Bang Theory and the evidence supporting it in the form of a rhyme/rap. Here's the start:

Big Bang singularity
Universal regularity
Space expanding
Attention demanding

Personal Reflection

Does the Big Bang Theory remove the need for a creator God?

This little sketch is based on a famous sketch involving John Cleese, Ronnie Barker and Ronnie Corbett (in The Frost Report) where three men explore the similarities and differences between their social classes (Cleese representing upper class, Barker middle class and Corbett working class). This version applies the same principle to the debate about the origins of the Universe.

Three people stand before you in a line. One is in the white lab coat of a scientist (1) and stands to the right. On his left is someone dressed in everyday clothes (2) and on his left is someone dressed in clothing which indicates that he is a Christian (3)...

2: *(looks first at audience)* I am an ordinary guy. I look to him *(looks at 1)* to explain how things work. He tells me about the laws of nature. He tells me that the Universe began with a Big Bang. I look to him *(turns to 3)* to explain what my life is for and to help me make sense of life's meaning.

1: I am a scientist. I tell him *(looks at 2)* that the laws of nature are the cause of everything and I tell him *(looks at 3)* that he has an imaginary friend.

3: I am a Christian. I tell him *(looks at 2)* that God made the Universe and I tell him *(looks at 1)* that even the laws of nature need a cause.

2: I get very confused. I think he *(looks at 1)* helps me to understand the way things happened but I think he *(looks at 3)* helps me to understand why they happened.

→

CHAPTER 7

What is the Origin of the Universe: are the Views of
Science and Religion Compatible?

1: I tell him *(looks at 2)* that the Universe began in a mighty explosion where all time and space began and I tell him *(looks at 3)* that this leaves no room for a God outside of space or time.

3: I tell him *(looks at 2)* that God can exist outside of space and time and I tell him *(looks at 1)* that nothing can cause itself.

1: I tell him *(looks at 3)* that if nothing can cause itself, then neither can God and I tell him *(looks at 2)* that if everything needs a cause then so does God.

2: I get very confused.

3: I tell him *(looks at 2)* that God is omnipotent and omniscient and so can do anything, including being uncaused and I tell him *(looks at 1)* that Big Bang theory is just as much an act of faith as anything.

1: I tell him *(looks at 2)* that God can't be both omnipotent and omniscient because then he could never change his mind and I tell him *(looks at 3)* that Big Bang theory isn't faith, I have evidence for it.

2: I get very confused. I ask him *(looks at 1)* why the Universe had to begin when it might as well not have and I ask him *(looks at 3)* why a God would have created it at all?

1: I tell him *(looks at 2)* that the Universe does not need a reason for its beginning, it just began, and I tell him *(looks at 3)* that it's just as likely that the Universe came into being out of nothing as that there is an even bigger being who always existed.

3: I tell him *(looks at 1)* that God created the Universe for a purpose and I tell him *(looks at 2)* that the purpose is known only to God.

2: I get very confused. I ask him *(looks at 3)* and him *(looks at 1)* why they can't just agree that they have different ways of explaining the same thing and why do I have to believe one or the other?

Talk Point   **25**

Do you agree that you have to believe in either the Big Bang or the creation of the Universe by God?

Three Interpretations of Scientific and Religious Explanations for the Origin of the Universe

As you know, the history of the relationship between science and religion – particularly between science and Christianity – is a messy one. As science grew and developed, it increasingly explained things which previously had been explained in 'religious' ways. Many new scientific developments seemed to challenge the very

What is the Origin of the Universe: are the Views of
Science and Religion Compatible?

CHAPTER 7

basics of religious belief. Scientists suffered ridicule, persecution and worse for proposing their theories, especially when those theories went against the view taught by the Church.

Nowadays, it is probably also true that there are religious people who suffer ridicule and 'persecution' (though not to the same extent as those early scientists) because they disagree with scientific theories about the origin of the Universe. They might be regarded by some as clinging onto explanations which have now been overruled by the findings of science. Is that the case? Are religious explanations for the origin of the Universe hopelessly out of date? Has science replaced religion as the way to explain the Universe in which we live? Can the two ways of looking at things ever exist side-by side? Well, of course, they do. As you know, there are scientists who are also religious people. There are even scientists and religious people who accept that *both* Big Bang theory and the creation of the Universe by God are true. Are they living with a hopeless contradiction or simply seeing things differently? Is the explanation for the origin of the Universe a simple either/or?

Source 29

Creation of the Universe by God

1   The Bible is the written Word of God. It is divinely inspired and inerrant throughout. Its assertions are factually true in all the original autographs. It is the supreme authority in all matters of faith and conduct.

2   The final guide to the interpretation of Scripture is Scripture itself.

3   The account of origins presented in Genesis is a simple but factual presentation of actual events and therefore provides a reliable framework for scientific research into the question of the origin and history of life.

Comment: This quote is from the Creation Science Movement. Its website explains its view that the Bible is right. Its argument rests on the literal truth of the Bible.

https://www.csm.org.uk/statement.php

Interpretation 1: The Big Bang Theory Contradicts Revelation, Rejecting Science

This interpretation of the issue of whether the Universe began with the Big Bang or through the creative action of a God has a positive and negative dimension. The negative dimension is that the theory and the evidence supporting the Big Bang is incorrect (or incorrectly understood) and the positive is that the explanation for the cause of the beginning of the Universe is already made clear in Christian scriptures. Christian literalists are most likely to support some of the views overleaf.

CHAPTER 7

What is the Origin of the Universe: are the Views of Science and Religion Compatible?

Big Bang Theory Is Wrong

◆ Much of the 'evidence' for the existence of the Big Bang is **theoretical**. It is based on complex and obscure mathematics and physics which most ordinary people (and some scientists probably) couldn't hope to understand. This means that we have to accept the conclusions of these mathematical and physical calculations without perhaps being able to check them for ourselves. Now, of course, we could go off and study them and learn then – so in principle at least they are understandable by everyone – but in reality they are 'held' by the maths and physics 'communities'. The important point however is that they are theoretical. No matter how many calculations you do and how complex they are, they still only point to a shadow of what must have been, not to the thing itself. Just because something is *almost certainly* theoretically true does not mean automatically that it is *actually* true.

◆ You know also from your study of scientific method that all scientific findings must be **interpreted**. This interpretation can lead to one thing instead or another, and the interpreting actually plays a part in deciding which conclusion is reached. So, working through the theory of the origins of the Universe as mathematical calculations alone, scientists will come up against points where they have to rely on the likelihood of one assumption being greater than another. This 'choice' may well be based on good reasons, but it can still be thought of as a choice – something instead of something else. Now, if you add to that, the fact that the scientist might have started off with the 'belief' that the Universe began with a Big Bang, then you have the possibility that one choice about the calculations might be made over another. This could result in mistakes and so reaching conclusions which another set of calculations would not support. In other words, believers in the Big Bang are more likely to notice, follow-up and report theoretical calculations which support the view that they started out with. The calculations will follow the **assumptions** and so a particular set of **conclusions** will be reached.

◆ The theoretical calculations upon which the theory of the Big Bang is based might also be *actually* wrong. With the Big Bang we're talking about an event of unimaginable force and a whole concept which is mind-bogglingly difficult to get your head round (the beginning of time – when?). Perhaps mathematical symbols and complex equations are just not up to the job. You've probably come across things in life where words just aren't up to explaining the thing – perhaps the maths just isn't up to explaining the Big Bang in any convincing way. Or perhaps it nearly is, but some of the calculations aren't and they have thrown the whole thing into a state of confusion – not secure enough to base an explanation of the beginning of everything on anyway.

◆ If we move from the theoretical
explanations to the ones based on
observable evidence, then we have
further problems. For example, the
expansion of the Universe seems to be
less **uniform** ('even') than was once
thought. Red shift shows slight
variations throughout the Universe –
why is this? Also, the background
radiation shows 'hotspots' and 'cooler'
regions – why is this? Now these
might just be blips in our
understanding, things which we've yet
to explain and will be able to soon,
but they might also be crucial
evidence that the Big Bang wasn't as
we thought… or that the Universe
came into being in some other way.

◆ Opponents of Big Bang theory will argue that the 'evidence' for the Big Bang is
simply one way of looking at and understanding what we see: that doesn't mean
that it is true. On the other hand, this sounds very much like a viewpoint that
you will come across in the next section called the '**God of the gaps**' theory.
This suggests that 'gaps' in scientific explanations can always be 'plugged' by
proposing the existence of a God. The trouble is as these gaps get 'smaller'
(through science explaining more and more) the 'gaps' available to fill with a
God become fewer and so 'filling' them with a God much less easy to defend.
However, those who oppose Big Bang theory may argue that the evidence, either
theoretical or empirical, is not strong enough yet to do away with the need for a
creator. In particular, they might point to the fact that, as yet, science has not
been able to explain why the Big Bang had to happen when it just as easily
might not.

The alternative view presented by Christians is a more positive one, and not simply
based on picking holes in scientific Big Bang theory. Instead it is based on the idea
that the Bible is right.

The Bible's Creation Story Is Right

This should take you right back to the discussions about scientific and religious
methods of explaining what is true. The Bible describes the creation of the Universe
as something which God did over six days. According to Christian literalists, if it's in
the Bible it is true because the Bible is the inspired word of God and something
which he personally sent us as guidance. The Bible does not speak of a Big Bang,
but instead of the creative action of a God. Therefore that is what happened. If the
Big Bang were true then the Bible would have told us about it. The Bible did not,
therefore it cannot be true.

CHAPTER 7

What is the Origin of the Universe: are the Views of Science and Religion Compatible?

For the literalist, accepting the truth of the Bible through faith is the key. If the scientific evidence seems to go against the Bible's teaching then you do as you would in the face of any challenge to your beliefs: you hold onto your faith. In this case that means believing in the biblical creation story, not the Big Bang, no matter how convincing the theoretical or observable evidence might seem. Besides which, for some Christian literalists there are scientific theories which could be interpreted as lending some support to their view. For example, the Hartle-Hawking theory suggests that there was no singularity at the 'beginning' of the Universe, the Universe just 'came to be' out of nothing.

Christian literalists believe that God created the Universe out of nothing and this has similarities with the Hartle-Hawking theory. To do this completely however they would have to also agree with Hartle-Hawking's implication that, therefore, God could not have existed 'before' the Big Bang because nothing could have. Literalists would, at this point, turn to the literal truth of the Bible as supporting the existence of God, and their belief that God is able to be 'outside of space and time'... because he's God.

The Bible's creation story is right

All members must subscribe to the following statement of belief:

1   The Bible is the written Word of God, and because it is inspired throughout, all its assertions are historically and scientifically true in the original autographs. To the student of nature this means that the account of origins in Genesis is a factual presentation of simple historical truths.

2   All basic types of living things, including man, were made by direct creative acts of God during the Creation Week described in Genesis. Whatever biological changes have occurred since Creation Week have accomplished only changes within the original created kinds.

3   The great flood described in Genesis, commonly referred to as the Noachian Flood, was an historic event worldwide in its extent and effect.

What is the Origin of the Universe: are the Views of
Science and Religion Compatible?

CHAPTER 7

4 We are an organisation of Christian men and women of science who accept Jesus Christ as our Lord and Saviour. The account of the special creation of Adam and Eve as one man and one woman and their subsequent fall into sin is the basis for our belief in the necessity of a Saviour for all mankind. Therefore, salvation can come only through accepting Jesus Christ as our Saviour.

Comment: The Creation Research Society is an organisation of scientists and lay people who fully believe in the creation as outlined in Genesis.

http://www.creationresearch.org/stmnt_of_belief.htm

Creationism and Creation Science/Intelligent Design

Creationism is based on the belief that the Bible should be taken as literal truth. The Bible describes the creation of the Universe in six days. There's no reason to doubt that those six days are six 24-hour periods, and that God created everything just as it is. There is no need for God to give us a scientific account of the creation as that's really his business not ours. He is the creator, not us and therefore our desire to want to know how he did it is another example of fallen mankind – humans trying to make themselves God, just like Adam did. Creationists do not need to tackle the scientific evidence, because they have no need of it. All the evidence which is required about the creation of the Universe is in God's holy word.

In the USA, **Creationism** is taught alongside Big Bang Theory in some schools and there are schools in the UK which want to start doing this too. Their argument is that presenting only the theory of the Big Bang (as happens in most schools in the USA) does not allow children to 'make up their own minds' based on all the alternative viewpoints. The USA, of course, has no RMPS in its state schools (it does in private schools but it's usually not the kind of RMPS you'd be familiar with). In Scotland, alternative views to the Big Bang are likely to be 'taught' and discussed in schools (you're doing it now after all) so the issue of only being taught the Big Bang theory does not arise here. In the USA there is a great debate about Creationism being taught in schools – Creationists think it should, because doing so recognises that not everyone accepts the Big Bang theory. Opponents however feel that schools are not the place to study such views because Creationism is not based on anything other than belief and goes against the demonstrated scientific evidence. The argument rolls on:

In addition to Creationism, there is also a movement which calls itself **Creation Science** – or the theory of

CHAPTER 7

What is the Origin of the Universe: are the Views of
Science and Religion Compatible?

'**Intelligent Design**'. This view takes a slightly different approach to Creationists
because it attempts to get into discussions about the science of the origins of the
Universe (and the development of life on Earth) on an even footing. It uses scientific
evidence to support the view that God created the Universe and challenges the
scientific evidence which suggests that there's no need for a creator. It argues that
much of the scientific evidence for the origins of the Universe is flawed and
therefore wrong, and it also argues that there is scientifically respectable evidence
which supports the creation of the Universe by God. You will come into contact
with this more fully in Area 3. Creation Science/Intelligent Design argues that there
is good solid *scientific* evidence to support the belief that God created the Universe
and that he did so for a purpose.

Scientific materialists are critical of creation science (some think of it as an
oxymoron – that creation and science are complete opposites which just don't go
together) because, in their opinion, creation science draws its own conclusions about
the scientific evidence and – in some cases it is claimed – comes up with rather
dubious evidence. However, Creation Scientists remain convinced that scientific
methods and evidence can be used to support their view that God created the
Universe and everything in it and that this evidence is every bit as convincing as any
other scientific evidence.

Talk Point

26

*Should Creationism and creation science be taught
alongside science in schools?*

Source 31

Is Intelligent Design the Same as Creationism?

No. The theory of Intelligent Design is simply an effort to empirically detect
whether the "apparent design" in nature acknowledged by virtually all biologists
is genuine design (the product of an intelligent cause) or is simply the product of
an undirected process such as natural selection acting on random variations.
Creationism typically starts with a religious text and tries to see how the findings
of science can be reconciled to it. Intelligent Design starts with the empirical
evidence of nature and seeks to ascertain what inferences can be drawn from
that evidence. Unlike Creationism, the scientific theory of Intelligent Design does
not claim that modern biology can identify whether the intelligent cause detected
through science is supernatural.

What is the Origin of the Universe: are the Views of
Science and Religion Compatible?

CHAPTER 7

Comment: This makes clear the difference between Intelligent Design and Creationism. Creationism starts and effectively ends with the truth of the Bible whereas Intelligent Design uses scientific method to support its view that God created the Universe.

http://www.intelligentdesign.org/whatisid.php

Source 32

Big Bang Theory is Wrong

'Down with the Big Bang'; 'The Big Bang Theory Goes Kerplooey'; 'The Big Bang Theory Explodes'; 'Sorry, Big Bang Theory is a Dud'; 'Map Challenges Theory of Universe'; 'Astronomers' New Data Jolt Vital Part of Big Bang Theory'; 'Quasar Clumps Dim Cosmological Theory'. These have been titles of a few of the articles found in newspapers and science journals in the last two or three years, as the Big Bang theory has received one body blow after another. And why not? We know that the Universe did not begin with a Big Bang – it will end with a Big Bang, for 'but the day of the Lord will come as a thief in the night; in which the heavens shall pass away with a great noise, and the elements shall melt with fervent heat, the Earth also and the works that are therein shall be burned up' (II Peter 3:10). Cosmologists have thus miserably failed as to the time, nature, and cause of the Big Bang.

Comment: Gish's article is on the website of the Institute for Creation Research and goes on to challenge most of the scientific evidence for the Big Bang concluding at the end of the article:

Eventually, all such theories will fail, for "in the beginning God created the heaven and the Earth" (Genesis 1:1). "The heavens declare the glory of God; and the firmament showeth His handiwork" (Psalm 19:1).

*Duane T Gish: The Big Bang Theory Collapses at
http://www.icr.org/article/big-bang-theory-collapses*

The arguments and scientific evidence for Intelligent Design are every bit as complex and scientifically constructed as the Big Bang theory. Supporters of Intelligent Design point out that many who believe in it are just as scientifically qualified as those who reject it. The detailed science itself is complex and for the purposes of your course in RMPS you need simply to know that this is not simply a debate between those with evidence and those with only faith – it is a debate which is also based on conflicting conclusions on the available scientific evidence – each one as firmly believed as the other.

CHAPTER 7

What is the Origin of the Universe: are the Views of Science and Religion Compatible?

Simple Section Summary

- ◆ The cause of the Universe is a key question for science and religion.
- ◆ If no creator was needed it questions the existence of a God.
- ◆ Christians might argue that:
  - The evidence for the Big Bang might be wrong.
  - It is based on assumptions and interpretations which might be wrong.
  - There is contradictory evidence which remains unexplained and these might leave 'room' for a creator God.
- ◆ Christian literalists and Creationists would add:
  - The Bible is the inspired word of God therefore its account of the creation is right (no Big Bang mentioned).
  - Supporters of Intelligent Design argue that there is scientific support for belief in creation by God.

Interpretation 2: Revelation Contradicts Big Bang Theory, Rejecting Religion

Again there is a positive and negative dimension to this.

Science is Right

Scientific cosmologists agree that the scientific evidence is in some ways **theoretical**. However they might point out that many scientific theories which were once theoretical were eventually supported with hard evidence once the means to do so was developed. So, although we may not have all the techniques to support the theory at the moment... it will come.

Although the calculations cannot point to the literal truth of the Big Bang, they are as close as it is possible to get (short of the development of time travel, and who knows...?) without actually being 'there' to witness it (which, if the theory is correct, would be impossible as there would be no*where* to observe it). So, in the same way that we rely on calculations of physical properties in many other aspects of our lives without having to 'prove' it, so too with the Big Bang. For example, we can accept the calculations that two rugby players travelling at speed towards each other will eventually stop in rather a spectacular smash – we wouldn't need to actually demonstrate it.

What is the Origin of the Universe: are the Views of
Science and Religion Compatible?

CHAPTER 7

Certainly, the calculations and observations require **interpretation** – but this is not blind guesswork. It is matching the best possible explanation to the evidence (theoretical or actual) available.

Of course mistakes can be made. That's why science always builds in **margins for error** in its claims (signified in calculations as ±). However, in relation to the calculations linked to the likelihood of the Big Bang, the possible errors are within accepted tolerance levels. Perhaps there is a sense in which the maths and physics can't fully explain the Big Bang (and might never be able to). But if that is so, why should anything else be able to explain it more fully (like religion)?

In short, many scientists argue that scientific explanations are our 'best bet' as a way of explaining the origin of the Universe – not a lucky guess by any means, but a pretty reliable explanation of what must have been – or at least as reliable as we're likely to get.

Religion is Wrong

This simply proposes that the Bible's explanation for the origin of the Universe is not something that should be understood literally. To say that a piece of writing (written by people long before the rise of modern science) could explain the origin of the Universe in scientific terms just doesn't make sense. If there was a God who did create the Universe, and he wanted us to believe that, why did he not give us more detail on the maths and physics involved? Did he really expect humans to accept a story of just a few lines to be an acceptable alternative to an understanding of the maths and physics involved in such a momentous process? Some scientists, like Richard Dawkins, will reject this in very strong terms, arguing that faith in the creation of the Universe by God is behaving in a way where your mind is so open that your brain is in danger of falling out. Others might simply argue that Christian

CHAPTER 7

What is the Origin of the Universe: are the Views of Science and Religion Compatible?

literalists and scientists can have no common ground here as one relies on the Bible as truth and the other doesn't – no more discussion required.

All of this means that the Big Bang removes the need for a creator of any kind and takes us back to Aquinas's cosmological argument. If the Universe began, as science claims, as a result of the laws of physics, then there is no need for any being to create it. The Universe is just a fact and no explanation for it is required – certainly not a religious one involving a God. This also removes the problem of who might have created such a being and is therefore a much simpler explanation (and science likes simplicity...honest). If religious people argue that God did not need to be created then by the same argument, the Universe didn't need to be created either. When you add to this the evidence in favour of the Big Bang and the corresponding lack of similar evidence for the existence of any divine being, then you have a simple solution: science is right and religion is wrong.

Source 33

Science as a Candle in the Dark

There is much that science doesn't understand, many mysteries still to be resolved... This may be the case forever. We are constantly stumbling on surprises... yet some New Age and religious writers assert that scientists believe that 'what they find is all there is'. Scientists may reject mystic revelations for which there is no evidence except somebody's say-so, but they hardly believe their knowledge of nature to be complete. Science is far from a perfect instrument of knowledge. It's just the best we have.

Comment: Sagan goes on to outline the many checks and cross-checks scientists put themselves through in their work – all to ensure that the evidence is as accurate as possible and he contrasts this with the approach of some 'New Age and religious writers' who seem to have no basis for their views other than that they think they're true.

Carl Sagan: The Demon-haunted world:
Science as a candle in the dark: Hodder Headline 1996 p29

What is the Origin of the Universe: are the Views of Science and Religion Compatible?

CHAPTER 7

Simple Section Summary

◆ Scientific materialists argue that the theory of the Big Bang is right and further evidence will be found.

◆ Interpretations of the evidence are not blind subjectivity, they are the best interpretations of the available evidence.

◆ The theory of and evidence for the Big Bang isn't perfect, but it's the best we've got.

◆ Scientific materialists also argue that we can't really take the Genesis account of the creation of the Universe seriously as it is not scientifically valid (nor was it meant to be understood that way).

◆ Therefore the Big Bang removes the need for a creator God.

Interpretation 3: Revelation and the Big Bang Theory Both Contribute to a Full Understanding of the Origins of the Universe

Christian Belief and Scientific Theory are Compatible

Put as simply as possible, this view suggests that science and Christianity are both right in their explanations of how the Universe began; it's just that their explanations are different – but not necessarily contradictory. Therefore they are both right but in different ways.

Source 34

Is the Big Bang Significant for Religious People?

The possibility of an unbounded finite past suggests that theological issues about 'the beginning' might best be [cut out of] theological discussions about creation. Since Augustine we have known that the ex nihilo tradition prefers to think of the creation of time and not creation in (pre-existing) time.

Comment: Russell uses the Hartle-Hawking proposal that the Big Bang had no 'beginning' as support for the belief that God created time, space and the Universe out of nothing. He argues that the scientific questions remaining about the Big Bang are possible openings for further dialogue between religion and science.

Robert John Russell: Is T=0 theologically significant?
In Science and Religion: History, Method, Dialogue: Routledge 1996 p219

CHAPTER 7

What is the Origin of the Universe: are the Views of
Science and Religion Compatible?

This interpretation can take many broad forms:

- *The NOMA argument* – as you saw in area 1, religion and science follow different methods which can lead to different conclusions. As long as neither tries to speak about things which rightly belong in the other **magisteria** then all will be well. Once religious people start making claims about science (as Creation scientists do), they are on dangerous ground because science works in completely different ways to religion. Scientific truth, for example, is founded upon evidence and experiment, whereas religious truth is more likely to be founded upon the revelation of God. In short, science and religion should stick to their own 'territory' and not cross over into each other's turf. Science and religion, like oil and water, don't mix and so we shouldn't try to make them.

This approach might lead to the view that:

- *Science explains the physical origin and development of the Universe* – science uses scientific methods to reach scientific claims. Scientific method is good at answering questions about the physical world. It can answer questions like 'How did the Universe begin?' with answers which explain the processes involved and the physical results which followed. Its theories and laws can explain physical properties as well as forces such as gravity and the behaviour of atoms. Scientific method uncovers the physical dimensions of our Universe, but that is as far as it goes. Scientific method can only test out the theories which are testable. It can only make claims about things which are, at least in principle, **verifiable** or **falsifiable**.

- If something is not verifiable or falsifiable using scientific method then perhaps science cannot say anything about it and, more importantly shouldn't. If science makes claims about things which are not able to be investigated (and therefore verified or falsified) by scientific method, then that's science going beyond its home ground and so any of its conclusions are no more valid than any others. For example, science can answer fundamental questions about how the Universe came to be – the physical forces which brought it into being, but... it cannot verify or falsify that the Universe was or was not brought into being by any divine being such as God. Therefore, if you like, the idea of God (and so the creation of the Universe by God) is *outside the reach* of the scientific method and so science cannot make any valid claims about God's existence or possible act of creation.

This is because:

- *Scientific method is not able to investigate or draw conclusions about spiritual matters* – Now what '**spiritual**' means could take up a whole book in itself, but for our purposes let's think of it as anything **non-physical**. Science deals with the physical Universe and it has neither the equipment nor the techniques to investigate anything non-physical (even whether the whole concept of 'spiritual' has any real meaning). This means that when discussing the origins of the Universe you could accept completely the Big Bang theory while still leaving room for creation by God. You could even, in principle, accept the initial conditions for the Big Bang – even if they suggest that the Big Bang caused itself

What is the Origin of the Universe: are the Views of
Science and Religion Compatible?

CHAPTER 7

– without having to rule out the existence of a God. This is all because no matter what the scientific findings *are*, they still *are not* able to prove or disprove the existence of a creator God because this is outside the scope of scientific enquiry.

Instead, Christians may argue that:

◆ *Christian revelation answers the important questions about the spiritual origins and goals of the Universe.* This ties in with the idea that the Bible is not a science book. Its purpose is completely different. Spiritual matters can only really be understood in spiritual ways, through revelation as in the religious method you examined in Area 1. Therefore Christians can, and do, live quite comfortably with the science of the Big Bang alongside religious beliefs about the purpose and goals of the Universe. They are not therefore necessarily opposites, but parallels – they run alongside each other without ever having to cross over or smash headlong into each other.

◆ *There is scientific evidence to support Intelligent Design.* This is the argument that a careful examination of all the available scientific evidence can lead to the conclusion that there is an intelligent designer behind it all. Creation scientists argue that they can accept many of the scientific claims related to the Big Bang theory, but that the evidence doesn't lead to the conclusion reached by scientific materialists – it leads to the conclusion that the observable evidence points to the existence of a creator God.

Looking at some of the more specific ideas, it's clear that religious people can hold on to their religious beliefs about the origin of the Universe *alongside* scientific explanations because:

◆ The biblical creation story need not be taken as literally true, but rather as a broader picture of the act of creation. Because the Big Bang is not specifically mentioned in Genesis 1 does not mean that it did not happen.

CHAPTER 7

What is the Origin of the Universe: are the Views of
Science and Religion Compatible?

- The biblical creation story does not intend to give a scientific explanation of the origins of the Universe. It simply exists to show that God created the Universe for a particular purpose.

- Accepting the biblical creation story is an act of faith – not the logical conclusion of scientific reasoning, as such it doesn't require scientific evidence or support.

In fact, the Big Bang might easily be the *mechanism* by which God created the Universe – perhaps a fairly unique moment where spiritual and physical briefly did 'cross over'. Why would there be any need for God to create a Universe in some *different* way to what we know about the Big Bang? Many early scientists, and some today, believe that the wonders which science continually reveals add to (rather than takes away from) their belief that God made it all. Maybe, the more detail that science reveals about the Big Bang, the more amazing God's work is seen to be and the more the Christian's beliefs are strengthened. This viewpoint could fit well with those who support Intelligent Design based on scientific evidence.

Finally, and of course, just as controversially, perhaps even if every single current and future scientific claim about the origin of the Universe in the Big Bang is 100 per cent true, what does that tell us about the **purpose** and **goal** of human life? What is life for? Now some scientific materialists might argue that 'life isn't *for* anything, it just is'. This might well be true, but then again it might not. Whatever views you have about religion, it is true that religion throughout its long existence has tried to grapple with this big (perhaps the biggest) question. Maybe the answer to this will be a scientific one, or maybe it won't. At any rate, perhaps it's difficult to argue that science or religion alone can answer such a question. This question of the origins, nature and possible purpose of human life is the subject of Area 3.

What is the Origin of the Universe: are the Views of Science and Religion Compatible?

CHAPTER 7

Source 35

Religion and Science

In the ongoing struggle of those of us who are both Christians and [scientific] theorists to bring our faith and our science into satisfactory equilibrium, the revisions required can go either way. Sometimes the best strategy is to revise something in our complex of Christian belief; but sometimes the best strategy is, on the contrary, to revise something in what science presents to us. For a variety of reasons, there is a deep tendency…in the West…to assume that in case of conflict between science and religion, religion has to give. But why should that be?

Comment: Wolterstoff is Professor of Philosophical Theology at Yale University. He argues that there are times when religion needs to adjust its beliefs and times when science needs to – it should not always be a one-way thing. This means that both must be flexible and open to alternatives.

Nicholas Wolterstoff: Theology & Science: Listening to each other in Science and Religion: History, Method, Dialogue: Routledge 1996 p103Pope John Paul II quoted in Carl Sagan: Billions and Billions p142

Simple Section Summary

◆ The NOMA argument suggests that you can believe in both the scientific and religious explanations for the origin of the Universe.

◆ Perhaps science explains the physical elements of the beginning of the Universe while religion explains the spiritual ones.

◆ Creation by God is perhaps outside the scope of scientific enquiry.

◆ Christian views do not answer scientific questions but they do answer questions about the meaning and purpose of human life which science does not (arguably).

◆ Christians can accept the Big Bang if they are prepared to accept that the biblical creation story is not literally true.

◆ Perhaps science and the Big Bang explains the mechanics of the beginnings of the Universe while Christian beliefs explain the meaning and purpose behind it all.

CHAPTER 7

What is the Origin of the Universe: are the Views of Science and Religion Compatible?

Activities

Knowledge, Understanding, Analysis and Evaluation

1 How might a Christian use the Genesis story to support Creationism?

2 Big Bang theory is very complicated – how might this lead to a Christian doubting it?

3 'Interpretation of the evidence is an important issue for scientific explanations of the origin of the Universe.' What does this mean and do you agree?

4 Could it be right that 'science isn't up to the job of explaining the Big Bang'?

5 Why is the idea of a 'God of the gaps' a possible problem for Christians?

6 In what way is faith important in reaching conclusions about the origin of the Universe?

7 Explain the views held by Creationists about the role of the Bible in this debate.

8 How does Creation Science differ from Creationism?

9 Why might some people reject the teaching of Creationism in schools?

10 Why do some scientists think Creation Science is an oxymoron?

11 What does Duane T Gish's quote tell you about his views on Big Bang theory?

12 What does it mean to say that scientific explanations of the Big Bang are our 'best bet'? Do you agree?

13 How might a scientific materialist argue against the Bible as a reliable source of information about the origin of the Universe?

14 How does the NOMA argument help religious people to 'live with' Big Bang Theory?

15 Do you agree that science cannot make any claims about 'spiritual' matters?

16 What do you think of the idea that religion and science are parallels?

17 'The Big Bang is the mechanism by which God created the Universe'. What does this statement mean? What opposite view of this might be given?

18 Do you think that, in relation to the origins of the Universe, science is based on fact and religion on belief?

What is the Origin of the Universe: are the Views of
Science and Religion Compatible?

CHAPTER 7

Active Learning

1 Have a class debate: 'The Big Bang theory of the origin of the Universe isn't completely accurate'.

2 Design a display/presentation on the beliefs of Creation Scientists about the origins of the Universe. You could do this in the form of a short video piece. You may need to use the internet to help you here.

3 Script a dialogue between a scientist who supports Big Bang Theory, a Creationist and a supporter of Intelligent Design.

4 Produce a poster with post-its which express the view of people in your class in response to the following statements:

If the Big Bang is true then this means…
If the Universe was created by God then this means…

5 Create two pieces of artwork and display them in your class. One should reflect the Big Bang Theory and the other the views of Creationists or Creation Scientists.

Unit Assessment Question

Higher:
'Big Bang Theory and Christian belief are completely compatible.' Would a Christian agree? **AE6**

Intermediate 2:
'You can either believe in the Big Bang or The creation story in Genesis.' Do you agree? Give reasons for your answer. **AE6**

Sample Exam Question

Higher:
'In relation to the origins of the Universe, science answers the 'how?' questions and religion answer the 'why?' questions.'
Is this an accurate view of the relationship between Christianity and Science? **AE10**

Intermediate 2:
'Christians can accept Big Bang Theory and remain Christians.' Do you agree? Give reasons for your answer. **AE8**

Homework

Creation Science/Intelligent Design has a number of websites related to this topic area. Look at some and produce two pieces of *scientific evidence* for the view that God created the Universe. You could start by looking at http://www.intelligentdesign.org which has links to other similar sites.

CHAPTER 7

What is the Origin of the Universe: are the Views of Science and Religion Compatible?

Personal Reflection

Some people think that the debate here about the origins of the Universe is one of the most important areas of discussion humans can have – because it is all about their origins and therefore 'who we are'. Others think that it is a pretty pointless area of discussion and that we should use our abilities instead to help make life better in the here and now. What do you think?

By the wonders of time travel, Ingledoink (Ing for short) from the planet Betrapudleioian has arrived a few hundred years after a crucial moment on a tiny little planet which they call Ziggly 3 – a planet which will soon go by the name of Earth. Ingledoink is making a TV documentary about his search for the Great Creator – an unbelievably powerful being who is regarded as the creator of all things across many galaxies where they're able to think about such things (they don't, for example, in the Arablat system because their bodies haven't been hooked up to their brains yet… but in a couple of trillion years things will be different). However, wherever he travels to and at whatever time in its past he arrives, he never quite seems to make it for the very first moment of life on that planet. He's sure his spaceship has been well serviced and that there's nothing really wrong with it, but no matter what, when he programmes in 'Year 0' for any of the planets he has visited on this quest, he always seems to miss it by several hundred years, and ends up interviewing one of the early inhabitants of whichever planet he's landed on. This inhabitant is always happy to tell him the story of the first life on that particular planet. Interestingly, there are some curious similarities between the stories told so far – from the Fiths of Garmudleon Minus One to the Crudges of the Big Helga spiral galaxy. On Ziggly 3/Earth, having missed the first moments of the planet by 920 years, he interviews a 15 year old human called Enosh, son of Seth.

Ing: So Seth, your Grandpa, Aidan – where did he come from?

Enosh: He was called Adam and he came from the Great I Am.

Ing: Otherwise known as God.

Enosh: Yip, that's the one. The name 'he who will be, who he will be': the 'Creator of all things'.

Ing: So after making everything else, God made Adam?

Enosh: He did.

Ing: Do you know how he did it?

Enosh: Yeah, I do, my dad told me everything – he's a 120 years old you know, but still kinda OK... for a dad... I suppose. Grandpa's all crashed out at the moment, having an old person snooze – well he is 920 years old after all, and never a day off work his whole life – well, after work... arrived that is, which is another story.

Ing: So I hear. So, how did Grandpa get here?

Enosh: Well the Creator had made all living things and then decided to finish it all off with something a bit more like Him – something He could kind of get to know if you like... have you tried having a chat with a turtle and... giraffes... they're so dull.

Ing: How did the Creator make Grandpa then?

Enosh: Well, I'm not really sure about the details, but I think He kind of shaped some dust and stuff and then sorta blew into it – up Grandpa's nose I think – yeah, I know, gross.

Ing: Then?

Enosh: The Creator and Grandpa did some gardening... boring.

Ing: So, how did Grandpa end up having kids?

Enosh: You don't know that? You've not had 'the talk' then?

Ing: It's a little different where I'm from... no, I mean how did Grandpa end up with a partner?

Enosh: Oh Granny you mean? She doesn't like to be called that though... 'Call me Ishshah sweetie' she always says – she's pretty cool for her age, and she's not had the easiest life so far, what with Uncle Cain and all.

Ing: Yes, he's in the land of Nod isn't he?

Enosh: We don't talk about him much – 'specially not to Granny.

Ing: So, you were telling me how Granny came on the scene.

Enosh: Oh yeah... well. All they tell me is that Grandpa fell asleep and when he woke up there was Granny.

Ing: Is that it?

Enosh: Well, there was something about cider, or apple-pie or something like that, and some pretty weird stuff happening in the woods – but they always say 'You'll hear about that when you're old enough to understand it' I mean, I'm 15 – how old do I need to be to understand things – they just treat me like a kid sometimes...

Ing: And the Creator?

Enosh: Well, He and Grandpa kind of fell out about the cider thing... and I don't think Grandpa hears much from Him these days...

Talk Point   27

What views are there in your class about the Adam and Eve story?

The Creation of Adam and Eve: Genesis Chapter 1

The Bible story of the creation of Adam and Eve – the first man and woman according to the Jewish scriptures – accepted by Christians (and Muslims) can be found in Genesis Chapters 1 and 2. In Chapter 1, God completes the creation of the Universe and the Earth and everything in it in six days. On the sixth day 'he created man and woman **in his own image**, in the image of God he created him' (Genesis 1:27). He then effectively tells them three things:

◆ They are to 'be fruitful and multiply and fill the Earth'. Which basically means have lots of babies (Genesis 1:28).

◆ That they are in charge of this whole world – they are given 'dominion' over all things (Genesis 1:28).

◆ They are given plants and fruits to eat (the first vegetarians?) (Genesis 1:29).

The Creation of Adam and Eve: Genesis Chapter 2

The second chapter of the Bible goes into a little more detail. Here, 'God formed man of dust from the ground and breathed into his nostrils the breath of life; and the man became a living being' (Genesis 2:7). God created a beautiful garden named **Eden**, and put **Adam**, the first man in it to look after it. Soon however, God decided, 'It is not good that

the man should be alone; I will make a helper fit for him' (Genesis 2:18), and so God created many living things – none of which seemed to be just right for Adam. So, 'God caused a deep sleep to fall upon the man, and while he slept took one of his ribs and closed up its place with flesh; and the rib which the Lord God had taken from the man he made into a woman and brought her to the man' (Genesis 2:21–22).

So, woman comes from man, which is reflected in the Hebrew words for man; 'ish' and woman; 'ishshah' (taken out of man). The scene described is of perfection; we still use the word 'Eden' as another word for 'perfect paradise' even today. The story tells of the first man and the first woman and how they were created specially by God and were the final act of the creation and the 'best bit' of God's creation. They are made, so the story says, in the image of God or as the story puts it; **'in our likeness'** (Genesis 1:26). One belief has it that the use of the word 'our' refers to the idea that God was discussing all this with the angels. No one is quite sure what 'in our likeness' means. Perhaps it has a physical meaning or perhaps a spiritual one. Perhaps this means that humans are 'god-like' in relation to how we physically look, or because of the abilities we have, or because we have a spiritual 'self' in a way which is similar to God.

However, what is important in the story for Christians is that life, including that of humans, originated on Earth because God made it happen. There's no implication that it was gradual or that any one living thing was linked to any other. They were made by God using physical material and, in the case of humans; they had life 'breathed into them' by God… end of story (well not quite).

The Creation of Human Life in Genesis 1 and 2: A Literal Interpretation

So, according to the scriptures, humans were created by God as the high spot of the creation of Earth and all the life on it. A literalist will accept the Genesis accounts of the creation of humans just as it is written. This is an act of **faith** – if the Bible says it happened then in faith you believe that it happened. The Bible is **God's word** and God's word is true. Even if the creation of a human from 'dust' seems hard to accept, a believer accepts it because it is in the Bible. Remember, Christians believe that God is all-powerful which means he can do anything – including making a fully functioning man from dust and a fully-functioning woman from the rib of a man.

Source 36

Literally Interpreting the Creation of Adam

Dismissing the first eleven chapters of Genesis as myths might seem a good idea at first. On reflection, a serious snag appears: the New Testament always refers to the early characters of Genesis, including Adam and Eve, as historical figures... Worse still, if we treat the fall of Adam as a piece of religious fiction we strike at the very heart of the Christian gospel... It is not surprising that liberal evolutionary theology has been a stepping stone to unbelief for some of its advocates.

Comment: Hayward argues that there is great danger in treating some of the Bible as fact and some as fiction. In particular with the story of Adam and Eve – where there are a lot of important Christian beliefs riding on it. Hayward points out that many of the New Testament's most important ideas are based on the belief that the story of Adam and Eve was true. He concludes that the possible end result of throwing out bits of the Bible when it suits you is that you may well eventually end up not believing in any of it at all.

Alan Hayward: Creation & Evolution: The Facts and the Fallacies;
Triangle 1985 p190–191

Young Earth Creationists

If you accept the Bible story of the creation of the Earth as literally true, then a rather interesting thing happens: you can work out the age of the Earth from the timescales in the Bible alone. All you need to do is work backwards through the family tree of Adam and Eve and count up all the various lifetimes. The total of all of these gives you the age of the Earth. There are some differences of opinion here about the exact age, but young age Creationists all agree that the creation of the Earth was only some **thousands** of years ago, rather than the **millions** of years proposed by science. We'll return to the arguments for and against Creationism/Creation Science in Chapter 10. For the moment, be aware that **Creationist Christians** accept the literal truth of the creation story in the Bible, including the creation of human life.

Cain's Wife – a Problem for Literalists?

In Genesis 4:8, it is said that 'Cain knew his wife, and she conceived and bore Enoch'. Those who argue against a literal interpretation of the creation story often use the sudden appearance of Cain's wife as a challenge to a literal interpretation of the story because: Adam and Eve had two sons, Cain and Abel. Cain killed Abel. Cain then found a wife – so either took his sister as his wife (a sister whose birth to Adam and Eve is not recorded) or there were other people created by God around the time of Adam and Eve (whose names are never recorded), two of whom were the parents of Cain's wife. Opponents of a literalist understanding of the creation story often use this as a big stick with which to bash literalists. Some literalists respond that these were different times so perhaps different rules applied about relationships or, that because the Bible *doesn't* mention the creation of other people in addition to Adam and Eve and their children is no reason to assume they *didn't* exist – and certainly no reason to doubt the overall truth of the story.

The Creation of Human Life in Genesis 1 and 2: A Symbolic Interpretation

Because of difficulties like the appearance of Cain's wife and the existence of a talking serpent (Genesis 3:1), not to mention the long life-spans of the first humans (Genesis 5:5) or the 'Nephilim' (sometimes translated as 'giants' – Genesis 6:4), many Christians now interpret the creation story symbolically. Without interpreting the story as symbolism and metaphor you would have to argue that a completely different set of conditions for living applied at the time, and you would have to explain why these are not the same now. This means accepting that God created humans, but that the story of Adam and Eve is a myth or a **metaphor** for the relationship between God and his creation. Instead of suggesting a factually true account of the origins of human life on Earth, the story in Genesis 1 and 2 is meant to convey the following ideas:

◆ God created the Earth and all its life forms.

◆ God created human life as a mixture of the **physical** and **spiritual.**

◆ God gave this creature the responsibility of ruling the world and all life on it.

◆ This creature was to know its place as a created being instead of a creator and form a special relationship with God.

◆ This being **disobeyed** God (by following its own will rather than God's).

◆ This event is called *the Fall* or sometimes as the idea of *original sin.*

◆ This disobedience led to consequences for man, woman and all creation.

◆ It is not important *how* God created humans, what is important is that he *did*.

Christians who interpret the creation of life on Earth symbolically also use faith to support their view. In their opinion, believing that the story is only symbolically true does not show a lack of faith, because you still need faith to 'fill in' some of the more obscure bits of the story (and to accept any part of it as true). They might also argue again that the story isn't meant to be a scientific explanation of the origin and development of life on Earth, but a story – a **myth** – with a message. This means that that story can *point to* truth even if it is not absolutely completely true in itself. There are three broad ways that you can interpret the story symbolically:

◆ It tells a story where none of the characters or the events were real. It is just a way to convey the important messages linked to the origin of human life in an understandable form.

◆ It tells a story which is partly true and partly exaggerated, focussing on one group of early humans (created by God) not all humanity.

◆ It reflects in story form, an actual (longer and far more complex) process of creation used by God and the gradual break-up of the relationship between God and his creation.

For some Christians, interpreting this story as symbols and metaphors means that you can accept the idea that the origin of human life is God. This can be done without getting bogged down in the fine details and possibly unknowable science.

Source 37

Different Christian Ways of Interpreting the Story

The doctrines of the Fall and original sin therefore come in for considerable revision. Orthodoxy insisted that the Fall was an historical event, a sin committed by a primordial couple from whom all subsequent human beings are descended: a quasi-biological transmission, as of an hereditary disease was envisaged. Liberal theology was compelled to revise this, for there was no way in which we could have evidence about the very first human beings so long before the invention of writing, and no way in which the human race could be traced back to an original couple... There was no evidence for a prehistoric Golden Age of mankind, and, what is more, the notion of original sin as a kind of hereditary disease, and as a mass punishment in perpetuity, was absurd.

→

Comment: Cupitt points out some of the contrasting views about the Genesis story within Christianity at the time of the development of evolutionary theory. He points out that there is a tension between literal interpretations of the story and more liberal ones.

Don Cupitt: Only Human SCM Press 1985 p45

Simple Section Summary

◆ Genesis Chapter 1 describes the creation of Earth and life on it.
◆ Adam and Eve are presented as the first humans.
◆ They are made in the likeness of God and a story follows which ends with their disobedience and banishment from the Garden of Eden.
◆ Christian literalists argue that the creation of humans in the Bible is literally true just as it is written.
◆ Therefore Creationists argue that the Earth is only a few million years old.
◆ Some Christians accept the Genesis creation story as allegory and metaphor. It has symbolic meanings about the relationship between the creator and his creation.
◆ Therefore the creation of humanity is not a scientific explanation but a story with a message.
◆ It therefore relates to spiritual matters not physical ones.

God as Designer: Paley's Teleological Argument

Supposing you're walking through your school dining room with a friend and you come across a plate on a table. On the plate is a steaming hot scotch pie topped with beans and some grated cheese. You turn to your friend and comment: 'Now, what do you think the chances of that are?' 'Eh?' your friend replies, you continue, 'A pie – topped with beans and cheese just appearing out of nowhere – the pie forming itself from the atoms in the air and being joined by the beans which fell from the sky dragging some unwilling cheese along on the way, scooping them right out of the ether – and then the mighty forces of nature at work in zapping it with some unknown radiation to heat it up… All nice and scrummy and ready for eating…'

By this time it would be surprising if your friend was within a mile or two of you, or rather – more likely – calling the school nurse. No, any reasonable person would assume that the pie, the beans and the cheese had all been made elsewhere, brought together, heated (quite recently) and set out to eat. More importantly, you would assume that this had been done by *someone*, and that it could not have happened without someone being involved in causing it. Pies, beans and cheese don't just appear fully formed, and their carefully formed structure must suggest an act of creation.

William Paley (1743–1805) came up with a similar argument, but not about pies. In Paley's day, watches were mechanical – full of intricate tiny little cogs and springs – and they would only work if they were all put together in exactly the right way, with exactly the right amount of tension and so on. Paley proposed that if you stumbled across a watch in a field, you would have to assume that someone had made it and that it had come from somewhere – one thing you would not be likely to conclude was that it just appeared spontaneously out of thin air – even if there had been millions of years available for all the pieces to independently come together into a fully functioning working watch. You would assume that it had been **created** and therefore that it had a **creator.**

Paley compared the watch to the Universe. He argued that the Universe, and all the varied life on Earth, was such a complex and complicated system that it could not have come together through **'blind chance'** and that therefore, just like the watch, the Universe must be created and have a creator. Now, creating a watch takes a bit of skill – because it's a complicated wee thing – so you need quite a clever person to make it just right: imagine how much more complicated the Universe is (not to mention big) and so how much more complex (and big and powerful) it's creator would have to be. Paley's argument was simple:

◆ In its complexity and grandeur, the Universe, Earth and life on it, is quite something.

◆ Such a thing could not have come together through blind chance.

◆ Therefore it must have a creator.

◆ Such a role can only be filled by a being such as God.

◆ Therefore God must exist and the Universe must be a created thing.

Paley's teleological argument (this is also called the **argument from design)** suggests that simply by looking around us we have to reach the conclusion that the world we observe must have had an intelligent designer who created it to be the way it is and (probably) with a purpose to it. Just as a watch exists 'for' something and couldn't have come about without a helping hand, neither can the Universe. Paley, and others who accepted his view, examined the complexities of the natural world and concluded that, just like a watch, the Universe seems ordered and structured in such a precise way that the only explanation for such precision is the existence of an **intelligent designer** God.

Other versions of the teleological argument make a distinction between two of its ideas. They talk about **design qua regularity**, which means that things seem put together in a way that makes sense and **design qua purpose** which means that things give the appearance of being designed for a particular purpose (which just happens to match up with their design).

Accepting the Teleological Argument (Argument from Design)

The argument is sound because it gives reasonable logical support to what the Bible teaches anyway – that God made the Universe, Earth and all its life for a purpose.

The probability of everything coming together in just such a perfect and balanced way by **chance** is just too ridiculous. No matter how long it took, nature, with all its intricacies and complexities cannot be explained as the result of chance factors. The teleological argument proposes a meaningful alternative:

◆ The conditions in place on planet Earth are just ideal for the existence of life.

◆ The more scientific discoveries we make, the more we find that the balance of life on Earth is just perfect for life.

◆ Such a precise balance seems unlikely to be the result of chance therefore it must be the result of Intelligent Design.

◆ The logical conclusion of the argument makes sense – only a God could have done such a thing.

Source 38

Paley on Lack of Perfection

It is not necessary that a machine be perfect in order to show with what design it was made: still less necessary, where the only question is whether it were made with any design at all.

Comment: Paley argues that even if a watch didn't always work properly, it is still something that was made. Perhaps the Universe looks (to us) as if it doesn't always work well, but as humans, how would we know if that were the case or not?

William Paley: Natural Theology 1800

Talk Point

28

What do you think of Paley's argument?

Rejecting the Teleological Argument Part 1

One argument against it comes from Immanuel Kant. He argued that the 'structure and order' we see in nature exists only in our minds and not in reality. No matter what kind of Universe we lived in, we'd always think that it was 'perfect' (no matter how different it was from what we have). Therefore the order and beauty of nature is just the way we see it, not how it is. So, we propose a God to solve the problem of how things are so perfect and ordered, but of course there is no problem to solve because things only appear perfect and ordered. Therefore, the teleological argument never really gets off the ground.

Another philosopher, David Hume really went to town on Paley's argument, coming up with no less than eight criticisms of it:

1 Maybe the Universe is designed exactly as Paley claims, but that doesn't prove that God (specifically the Christian God) created it. It could be any kind of being that did the work.

2 Maybe there was more than one God – or maybe God designed it and then ceased to exist.

3 An *argument* that the Universe is designed is not the same as *proof* that it was designed.

4 The existence of a designer just begs the question 'who designed him?' (See Cosmological Argument discussion in Area 2).

5 Even if it was designed by a designer, it still tells us nothing about him (or her, or them).

6   If God made himself, why can't the Universe have done so too? (Or if God has always existed without a beginning why can't the Universe do the same?)

7   Maybe the laws of physics are 'God'.

8   The Universe, planet Earth and life on it aren't exactly perfect by any stretch of the imagination – how does this point to a designer?

Rejecting the Teleological Argument Part 2

◆   According to Paley, the Universe is perfectly organised and therefore must have been designed. But remember, this 'perfection' is just how we see it. A peaceful grassy riverbank on a summer's day might look pretty and perfectly balanced, but look more closely and you'll see a fairly violent scene instead – with insects of all kinds gobbling each other up and generally acting very 'nastily'.

◆   The Universe, planet Earth and life on it seems to **require pain and suffering** – which seems like a rather odd design. Just think, your survival depends completely upon the death of other living things (plant or animal) and try telling a newborn baby zebra that the world is perfectly designed as the lion sinks its teeth into its neck, bringing its short life to a violent end.

◆   The Universe also seems to be a place where **luck**, rather than order and structure is king. In life it just seems that sometimes you can be in the wrong place at the wrong time (or the right place at the right time of course) – it all seems a bit 'hit or miss' and certainly not the creative action of a God who knows what he's up to.

◆   We can't really argue that because conditions seem just right for life on Earth that it points to a creator for two reasons: firstly the life we have is related to the conditions, if there were different conditions there might be different life forms; Secondly, it suggests that Earth exists somehow mainly for human benefit. This idea, called the **anthropic principle** seems a little… well… arrogant.

Source 39

Rejecting Paley's Argument

When you come to look into this argument from design, it is a most astonishing thing that people can believe that this world, with all the things that are in it, with all its defects, should be the best that omnipotence and omniscience has been able to produce in millions of years. I really cannot believe it.

Comment: Russell, a famous atheist wonders whether this world was the best God could have come up with and suggests that most people, given the power, could have done a better job.

Bertrand Russell: Why I am not Christian: Unwin 1979 p18

Simple Section Summary

◆ William Paley proposed the teleological argument.
◆ This says that just as a watch is created by an intelligent designer so too must the whole Universe be created.
◆ This argument says that the whole Universe shows evidence of order and design. This could not have happened by chance and requires a very powerful intelligent designer which must have been God.
◆ David Hume opposes Paley's argument by claiming that, among other things, it does not have to point to the Christian God, nor does it prove that he still exists.
◆ Hume argues that the teleological argument fails logically.
◆ Others argue that it fails because nature's design is not full of beauty and order but chaos and ugliness which points either to no creator or a very confusing one.

Special Intermediate 1 Interlude

Pretty much all of the course material you have looked at so far, and all that's to come, is also in the Intermediate 1 Unit: Existence of God. However, there is a special section which only Intermediate 1 candidates get to do and this is it. If you're not doing Intermediate 1 you can skip all of this (jump to page 148!) or read it anyway because you're a dedicated and committed student who never tires of learning new stuff… If you are doing Intermediate 1 there's even more on this topic in the textbook called *Nature of Belief* so get your teacher to buy some copies of that.

Talk Point 29

Does the existence of evil and suffering prove there's no God?

Evil and Suffering

For many people the existence of evil and suffering in the world is a very strong challenge to belief in God. The argument goes something like this:

◆ God is **all-knowing** – this means that he knows everything that has ever been as well as everything that is going to be. He knows exactly what you're doing right now as well as exactly what you're thinking.

◆ God is **all-powerful** – this means that God can do anything. His power is without limit and he can even break his own rules (like the laws of nature) if he wanted to.

◆ God is **all-loving** – this means that God cares for everything and everyone equally, it doesn't matter how big or small the thing is (or how good or bad) he loves it anyway.

◆ There is evil and suffering in the world – that's a fact.

◆ If God is all knowing then he must know about this evil and suffering – even the terrible things that haven't happened yet.

◆ If he is all powerful then he must be able to stop any evil and suffering no matter what the cause of it is.

◆ If he is all-good, then surely he must want to stop evil in whatever form it appears.

◆ Evil and suffering still happen.

◆ THEREFORE God must either not know about it, in which case he's not all-knowing, OR unable to stop it in which case he's not all-powerful OR unwilling to stop it, in which case he's not all-good.

◆ So, EITHER God isn't these things OR he doesn't exist.

The Nature of God

Evil and suffering are a particular challenge to belief in God because they are things which we can see and experience directly, whereas belief in God is most often based on pure faith (though of course many do claim and have claimed both to see and experience God). The existence of evil seems particularly difficult because Christians argue that God has additional important qualities. These qualities don't seem to match up with the existence of evil and suffering:

◆ God is **just**: This means that God is fair. The baddies get punished and the goodies get rewarded. However, evil doesn't seem to work that way. It sometimes seems as if evil is very **indiscriminate** – it affects people no matter what their lives are like. It is often said that 'the good die young' – which may or may not be true. However, it's obvious that people who suffer aren't always the people we think 'deserve' to suffer. Suffering seems to happen to people no matter how good or bad their lives are. Christians respond to this by saying, for example, that eventually the good are rewarded and the wicked punished. Christians believe in **judgement after death** and in an **eternal life.** At this judgment, Christians believe, those who deserve punishment will get it and those who deserve reward will get it.

This links to the next belief about God:

◆ God is **compassionate.** God cares in other words. Now looking at the bad things which happen in the world today a non-religious person might question this, but Christians respond by arguing that God shows compassion to those who suffer. For example, when someone is suffering, others usually rally round to help and show kindness – in fact, Christians argue, some of the greatest acts of kindness which humans ever experience are during times of suffering and troubles rather than when things are going well. Now, if you're suffering this is probably not much of an argument to hear and it's not likely that a Christian is going to say to you, "Now, don't worry about your pain and suffering, it's giving others a chance to be nice". However, the two do seem to go together sometimes. Also, Christians argue, God may be showing compassion in ways that we don't even understand or appreciate. Some Christians talk about the value of suffering as the idea that it makes us reflect upon our lives more clearly than we have ever done before. In so doing, perhaps we become the person we were always meant to be. Again, maybe not much comfort when you are suffering but who knows?

◆ Christians argue that God understands things in ways that we can't. Perhaps suffering and evil are things where we just have to hang on and have faith. God is **merciful**. God forgives and forgets. Some say that as a person gets close to death – what may have been terrible pain and suffering seems to give way to a sense of peace and calm. Now this could simply be a natural biological process or, it could be the action of a loving God showing mercy. Also, after death, your judgement will reflect your life and here's where mercy comes into its own according to Christian belief. Your eternal life could either be in the eternal presence of God (heaven) or in the eternal absence of God (hell). Which one you end up in will depend upon the circumstances of your life. However, if you accept God even in your dying moments, then he will forgive you for anything that you have done in your life and you will be accepted into heaven and judged compassionately. Of course, this is a belief and so difficult to balance up for some against the obvious reality of evil and suffering in life. But for Christians it is partly a response to the existence of evil and suffering.

For some, these qualities of God don't seem to match up with the reality of evil. How can God be all of these things and yet allow evil to happen? Is evil really a challenge to the very existence of God? Could a God with all of these properties really exist? The solution for many Christians is to put the ball back in our court – God isn't the cause of evil and suffering, we are.

Evil and Suffering Does Not Challenge the Existence of God: The Fall of Adam

An important part of the Genesis creation story is called the **Fall**. In the story, Adam and Eve are given a perfect place in which to live – the Garden of Eden. This is perfect in every imaginable way. They are given all that they need to live, as is every other living thing. There is even a suggestion in the early part of Genesis (Genesis 1:29–30) that every living thing is to exist on a vegetarian diet – which would certainly cut down a lot of the suffering of living things to provide food for other living things. However, all is perfect. All that Adam and Eve are not permitted to do is 'eat from the tree of knowledge of good and evil' (Genesis 2:17). In the story however, a serpent appears, understood by Christians to represent the devil,

and persuades Eve to eat from this tree of knowledge. His clinching argument for Eve is that God doesn't want them to eat from this tree because then they themselves will be god-like. Eve then persuades Adam to disobey God by eating from the tree and that's the Fall (from the grace of God).

Quite simply after this disobedience God punishes Adam and Eve. Adam is now to toil and sweat to survive, Eve is to experience great pain in childbirth, the serpent is to slither on its belly and so on. These specific punishments reflect the fact that Adam and Eve were now to be kicked out of the Garden of Eden and life would never be the same again – for them or for anything. And now, the important bit: Christians believe that Fall resulted in **Sin** coming to Earth. This sin was Adam and Eve's but it affected every part of creation. The perfection that existed in the Garden of Eden was now lost and **all creation was fallen.** In this way, evil and suffering entered the world and remains. It was not God's doing but the will of his creation – so we can't really blame God for suffering and evil because we brought it by our disobedience. When you add to this that all through the Bible God tries to get the relationship between him and his creation right again, it might seem a little unfair to blame him for the existence of suffering and evil, or to use suffering and evil as a challenge against his existence. All through history humans, and all creation, would bear the consequences of this fall in having to face the fact of suffering and evil.

Talk Point 30

What is free will?

Evil and Suffering Does Not Challenge the Existence of God: The Free Will Defence Argument

Linked to the fall in some ways this argument does not depend on the Bible story, but on a philosophical argument. It's quite simple really and goes like this:

◆ For God, freedom is one of the most important gifts he gives to his creation.

◆ Freedom means we can choose whatever we want to do… freely.

◆ If God did not allow us this freedom then we would just be robots, doing his will and we might as well not exist for all the independence we had.

◆ HOWEVER, this freedom can lead to good choices or bad ones.

◆ God MUST allow the **consequences** of our free will to take place (because if he does not then we're not really free).

◆ So, even if God does not like the consequences of our free choices he has to let them happen to safeguard our freedom – that's the price he pays (and we do too of course).

◆ So Evil and Suffering have to exist if we are to be free.

Here's an illustration: suppose you decide to do something 'bad'. Just as you do it, a great voice comes from the sky and says 'Oh no you don't' and a great hand comes from the clouds stopping your actions. Now what kind of world would that be? Actually, *a completely meaningless one.* This is because you could now do anything and just wait for God to jump in and stop it at just the right moment. No, that would be a crazy world. We all have to know that if we choose an action we have to live with its consequences – that's what free will is all about. So, bad consequences are just built into the system, they are the price we pay for being completely free.

Source 40

Free Will Defence

My general conclusion then, is that this world with all its unjust and apparently wasted suffering may nevertheless be what... Christian thought affirms that it is, namely a divinely created sphere of soul-making... Let us suppose that God creates finite persons to share in the life which He imparts to them. If He creates them in his immediate presence... they will have no creaturely independence in relation to their Maker. They will not be able to choose to worship God... A world without problems, difficulties and perils would be morally static. For moral and spiritual growth comes through response to challenges; in a paradise there would be no challenges...

Comment: Hick is a Christian who has possibly written more about the problem of evil than any other Christian. He argues that evil is necessary to safeguard freedom, but also that it provides humans with the challenges they need to grow morally and spiritually. God could stop evil but then we would have to believe in him and faith would no longer be needed.

John Hick Evil and the God of Love (2nd edition) London 1977 p336

Some Objections to These Arguments

◆ Whether the Fall is a symbolic story or a real event it does present us with some problems. Why should Adam and Eve have been punished for making free choices? It was hardly fair to tease them like this and then react so strongly to their choice. Why give them free will and then punish them for using it? Also, God created the serpent – why? Perhaps if there had been no smooth-talking serpent then they might never have disobeyed God.

◆ Wasn't the punishment a bit harsh? Whatever happened to God's forgiveness? Fair enough to punish Adam and Eve, but why all creation for the choice of two beings? And why for all time?

◆ Couldn't God have foreseen their choice? If he's all-knowing then he must have known that they were going to disobey and so could have saved himself the whole sorry affair in the first place.

◆ And what about the Free Will argument: why is free will far more important than anything else (or so it seems)? Is it really fair and right for someone to suffer terribly just so that the idea of free will is protected? Couldn't God let us exercise our free will *and* let the consequences happen, *but also* protect the innocent from unnecessary suffering? It seems a very weak defence to say that terrible suffering is necessary to protect free will.

◆ Christians respond to these challenges in many ways, but generally it comes down to a couple of things: humans are free beings – that is God's gift and something to be treasured. Unfortunately, it can result in harmful consequences (and did at the Fall), however, that's the way things are and we just have to accept it in faith. Free Will is central to what it means to be human – take away free will and you take away our humanity – one goes with the other and that's that.

Talk Point

31

What do you think of the Free Will argument?

Evil and Suffering Does Challenge the Existence of God: Suffering through Nature

Meteor strikes, floods, earthquakes, tsunamis, lightning strikes, hurricanes, freezing temperatures, heat waves, bacteria, bugs, disease, viruses, flu… on and on it goes. Sometimes it seems like planet Earth is a fairly dangerous place to be – a place where we're always at the mercy of Mother Nature and her mood swings. Now, you can't use the freewill argument to get God off the hook here – because volcanoes don't have free choices, they just do what they do, as do hurricanes and all other kinds of things referred to as **natural evil**. Here, the word evil doesn't really mean the same thing as it does when we talk about a murderer because nature isn't evil or good, it just is. Some call it **morally neutral** which means that the evil which results from natural disasters has nothing to do with anything other than natural forces doing their stuff. Here, the existence of God is again challenged by some who argue that he wouldn't allow these random things to happen with the devastating consequences that they bring. If he was there he'd stop them –

especially as this wouldn't harm anyone's free will…

Or would it? You could, of course, just stop there and claim that the existence of natural evil proves there is no God, because if there was a God then the world he created would be a lot less dangerous and cause a lot less (potentially no) suffering. Or we could still have earthquakes and volcanoes but God would quietly direct their harmful effects away from us… without us ever even knowing about it. However, he doesn't – so what's going on? How do Christians explain natural evil?

Natural evil is part of the natural physical forces which exist on Earth. These forces have to work out the way they do. What would be the point in God making the laws of nature and then cancelling them out every time they threatened to cause some harm. Nature must be able to act according to these natural forces without any interference from God. A world where this didn't happen would be an unpredictable world where nothing much would make sense.

Humans do have a part to play in at least some natural evil. People around the world still choose to live where they know nature sometimes causes problems. People live in the shadow of great volcanoes and on top of fault lines, they live where flash floods are common and in places where weather events sometimes take a turn for the worst. It's hardly fair then to blame God for our own choices. If you live on the slopes of a volcano you can't really complain should the volcano have the cheek to erupt – and it would be doubly cheeky to blame God for your dopey choice of place to live.

However for many people, the existence of evil is a serious challenge to the existence of an all-powerful, all-knowing and all-loving God. If you accept the argument that God won't interfere in natural events where suffering might be caused, and that he also doesn't interfere where humans cause evil and suffering then you are left with a God who just stands back and watches. For some, this can seem like quite a disinterested God and not a being who is involved in the lives of his creation. Christians respond by saying that God has tried throughout the history of humanity to get our relationship back on track and he can't be blamed because he lets us get on with it – that's not the action of a disinterested remote God, it's the action of a truly loving God.

Talk Point 32

If there's a God, should he make himself more obvious to us?

Simple Section Summary

- ◆ Evil and suffering exist.
- ◆ The fact that they do exist suggests that God is unwilling or unable to stop them.
- ◆ Therefore he's not much of a God or he doesn't exist at all.
- ◆ God being just, compassionate and merciful, as believed by Christians, doesn't match up with the existence of evil and suffering.
- ◆ Christians might argue that evil and suffering are mankind's fault.
- ◆ They were brought into the world by the disobedience of Adam and Eve at the fall.
- ◆ Another Christian argument is the Free Will defence.
- ◆ This says that humans have to be free in their actions, therefore if they choose to do wrong, God has to 'let them'.
- ◆ Therefore human-caused evil and suffering is a result of human free will and not God's choice.
- ◆ Opponents argue that humans could appear free while God could still stop them doing bad things.
- ◆ They also wonder why freedom might be more important than stopping suffering.
- ◆ Natural evil is not the result of human choices (it would appear) so perhaps it threatens the existence of a loving God.
- ◆ Christians argue that it does not because the laws of physics are not evil – they are neutral.
- ◆ Besides which, humans have the ability to understand nature and to live in ways which avoid its harmful effects (to an extent).
- ◆ Some Christians argue that the existence of evil and suffering is caused by the Devil.
- ◆ Some Christians argue that suffering has positive outcomes too – in helping people become better, stronger people (spiritually-speaking).

End of Intermediate 1 Interlude

Intelligent Design: The Arguments... Coming Soon

So far, we have only examined the claim that the origin of human life is that it was created by God through examining biblical writings and philosophical ideas. Creationists – generally speaking – argue that the evidence in the Bible is enough to conclude that God had life on Earth. However, Creation Scientists, also known as supporters of Intelligent Design, go further than this: they argue that there is reliable scientific evidence that the Universe, and life on Earth including humans, was created by an intelligent designer. However, before we examine their views in Chapter 10, we must explore the dominant scientific theory about the origin and development of life on Earth (including humans of course) as proposed in the 19th Century by Charles Darwin in his theory about evolution through natural selection. Many of the claims of supporters of Intelligent Design can only be properly considered once you understand what Darwin's theory is all about.

Activities

Knowledge, Understanding, Analysis and Evaluation

(NB *italics* refers to Intermediate 1 tasks only)

1 Describe the creation of human life according to Genesis 2.

2 What three things did God tell Adam and Eve?

3 According to the story, why did God create Eve?

4 What do people understand by the idea that humans were created 'in the image of God'?

5 What do Creationist Christians believe about the story of Adam and Eve?

6 Does Cain's wife present a problem for people who understand the creation story literally? Discuss both sides of the argument here.

7 In what way is faith important for those who understand the creation of Adam and Eve as literally true?

8 What are the important messages in the story of Adam and Eve for those who understand the story symbolically?

9 In your own words, describe William Paley's teleological argument.

10 Outline two views which support Paley's argument.

11 Explain three of David Hume's criticisms of the teleological argument.

12 Which of Hume's arguments (if any) do you think is the most challenging for the teleological argument?

13 Explain fully, with supporting reasons, your own views on Paley's argument.

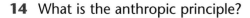

14 What is the anthropic principle?

15 Does the (apparent) appearance of design in nature prove that there is a creator God? Explain your answer.

16 *Christians believe that God is all-knowing, all-powerful and all-loving. What do these ideas mean?*

17 *How might the existence of evil challenge the existence of God?*

18 *In what way is the indiscriminate nature of evil a particular challenge for belief in God?*

19 *Would a compassionate God allow suffering? How might a Christian argue that he would?*

20 *What was the Fall?*

21 *How might the Fall explain the existence of evil?*

22 *In your own words, explain what is meant by the free will defence.*

23 *Do you think the free will defence argument works? Explain your answer.*

24 *How might a person challenge the Fall as the cause of suffering and evil in the world today?*

25 *What is the difference between natural evil and human evil?*

26 *Does it make sense to call natural evil…evil? Explain your answer.*

27 *In your opinion, does the existence of evil (natural and/or human) prove that there is no God?*

Active Learning

1 Use the Ingledoink interview in the stimulus and write a similar interview Ingledoink has with Adam which covers the events surrounding the Fall.

2 Illustrate the main points of the creation story in Genesis 1 and 2.

3 In the form of a rhyming poem, explain how a literalist interprets the creation of Adam and Eve. Here's the first two lines for you:

  • *You may think it's absurd, but it's clear in God's word*

  • *There was Adam and Eve, so you'd better believe…*

4 Have a class debate: 'The appearance of Cain's wife is a serious challenge for those who believe in the creation story in the Bible'.

5 Take a well known tune (such as 'she'll be coming round the mountains') and write some lyrics which explain the views of someone who understands the Genesis creation story as symbolism/metaphor.

6 Create a short illustrated information leaflet outlining Paley's teleological argument.

7 Create a display in your class which shows 'good' and 'bad' design in nature.

8 Write a short speech based on the responses of David Hume to Paley's teleological argument.

9 *Find newspaper and magazine articles about suffering and evil in the world today. For each one, think about how a Christian might explain them based on what you know about their response to the problem of evil.*

10 Create an illustrated display entitled
'The free will argument'.

11 Design, carry out and report your
findings on a survey which explores
people's beliefs about evil, suffering and
how they might affect belief in God.

Unit Assessment Question

Higher:
Why do some Christians think that you
must accept the story of Adam and Eve as
literally true? **AE4**

Intermediate 2:
Explain ONE way in which some
Christians explain the origin of life. **KU4**

Intermediate 1:
Does the existence of evil and suffering
prove there's no God? **AE4**

Sample Exam Question

Higher:
'You cannot be a Christian if you do not
accept that there really was an Adam and
an Eve.' Do you agree? **AE6**

Intermediate 2:
Explain what a Christian would mean
by a 'literal interpretation of the creation
story'. **KU4**

Intermediate 1:
Explain what Christians mean by the Free
Will defence. **KU4**

Homework

Do internet searches on 'beliefs about Adam and Eve'. Write a
report of the sites you visit and the range of views held.

*Do internet searches on 'The Free Will defence argument'.
Write a report of the sites you visit and the range of views held
about the argument.*

Personal Reflection

Does the world in which you live point to the probability that
there is a God or that there is not?

CHAPTER 9 | What is the Origin of Human Life: Human Life Emerged as a Result of the Process of Evolution?

There once was a fellow called Darwin,
who had the great cheek to believe
that all life on our world just developed,
with no need for an Adam or Eve.

He argued for natural selection,
that nature chose what lived or died,
no God was needed throughout this,
thus; 'Oh dear' some holy men sighed.

His evidence started with fossils,
dead creatures locked up in the rocks
'But surely that was the flood?'
said the holy men in the frocks.

And then there's vestigial organs,
ghosts of a previous try,
appendix and coccyx redundant
or wings that don't help things to fly.

Moreover there's various creatures
who live far away from the zoo,
like ostriches, koalas and emus,
but sadly no French kangaroo.

So off he went on a mission
to show that his theory was right,
on HMS Beagle – no cruise ship –
where he saw some incredible sights.

The finches that had the right beaks
to eat nuts that were lying around,
the tortoise with just the right hump
to reach food which was high off the ground.

He knew that some process occurred
that favoured such random mutation,
but DNA hadn't arrived yet
to ease poor old Darwin's frustration.

Darwin's bad health didn't help him,
and soon to his ending he went,
but not before he'd made us humans
match our chimpanzee cousins' descent.

If Darwin was still here today
he'd need bodyguards and protection
for still his theories cause trouble
most notably 'natural selection'.

CHAPTER 9

What is the Origin of Human Life: Human Life Emerged
as a Result of the Process of Evolution?

Setting the Scene for Charles Darwin

The theory of evolution by natural selection will
always be linked to the name of **Charles
Darwin**. Interestingly, the most widely used
image of him is the one with the very long
beard and him looking very old indeed.
However, his theory was put together long
before that, when he was just a young man in
fact. Also, his theory didn't just appear out of
the air, it was linked to many other scientific
discoveries and theories which were around in
his day. Darwin hadn't been all that interested
in studying at university and started off one
career after another – eventually he ended up
on board a ship, *The Beagle*, travelling
around the world. It was on this ship that he
really started to get to grips with his theory,
but many of his ideas were based on things he learned while
pottering around in his garden in the Kent countryside afterwards.

Also, Darwin wrote loads of letters to all sorts of people. These were not of the idle
chit-chat variety, but letters asking (some say pestering) others for information and
data which Darwin would build into his developing theory. Darwin also read about
discoveries and theories of the day in a wide variety of areas of science. Again,
many of these found their way into his own theory of evolution by natural selection.
Some of the theories and discoveries which he thought linked to the origin and
development of life on Earth were as follows:

◆ *The geological and fossil records*: the Earth's
history is locked up in its rocks. Layer upon
layer of rocks and the **fossilised life forms**
within them, suggested that there were living
things once on the Earth which were no
longer here (e.g. dinosaurs). It also seemed
to point to the idea that as time went on,
organisms became more and more
complex. Now, in Darwin's day most
people believed in the Genesis creation
story and these geological discoveries
raised some questions about it. For
example, why do some forms of life seem
to have 'died out'? Some explained this as
the result of the global flood which is
described in Genesis (the one with Noah's
Ark). However, the common idea of the
time – which thought of the history of the Earth

What is the Origin of Human Life: Human Life
Emerged as a Result of the Process of Evolution?

CHAPTER 9

itself as a series of **catastrophic** events (like floods) was being replaced with the theory that changes to the Earth throughout time were **gradual**. The geologist Charles Lyell was one of the leading geologists of his day and his theory of gradual change to the Earth's rocks was becoming widely accepted. Of course, you can imagine that once that idea had become accepted, it would be an easy leap to imagine that there had been some kind of development in life too – as Darwin came to propose. If the fossil record showed gradual change and occasional extinctions then it called into question any idea that God had created things at the beginning as they are now and evolution could take shape.

◆ *Vestigial organs*: Advances in biology and anatomy were showing that certain living things had what could only be described as organs which looked as if they should do something but don't. For example,

some insects have small wings which they don't use for flying. Why are they there? It began to seem to some that the idea that God would create an animal and give it some completely useless organ didn't make much sense. Perhaps a better explanation was that the organ once had a function but didn't any more – supporting the idea that life changed over time. Some religious people simply argued that just because humans can't see a 'reason' for an organ in a body, doesn't mean that there isn't one – perhaps God has a reason for it unknown to us.

◆ *Common features across species*: Humans have a ribcage, so do lions. The human hand is not that different from that of a chimpanzee. In fact, if you look across all the parts of the natural world you will find great similarities between species. This

led some to wonder whether there was some kind of relationship between different species, one which had branched apart at some time in the past. Again, religious people argued that there was nothing wrong with God using a similar design across a range of species, this made perfect sense – in fact it was a good use of nature to re-use an idea across species. However, for those who were beginning to question the Genesis account of creation it was yet another question mark: common features across species implies that they are related rather than created specially and uniquely.

153

CHAPTER 9

What is the Origin of Human Life: Human Life Emerged
as a Result of the Process of Evolution?

◆ *Breeding programmes*: In Darwin's
day, the basics of plant and animal
breeding were fairly well
understood. Farmers knew that
each species had a variety of
versions and that you could 'select'
the version of animal you wanted
and breed it so that you produced
more of that kind. You'd keep
picking the offspring that looked
the way you wanted them to and
breed from them and so you
were 'selecting' the qualities you
wanted in an 'unnatural' way. Again, this could raise a
question about what part God might play in all this. If God created everything,
it seemed as if humans could interfere in this by pushing things along the way
they wanted them to go.

◆ *Food supplies and populations*: Even in Darwin's day, it was known that
animal numbers were reduced in times of lack
of food (humans too, as great
famines caused many deaths –
as did particularly harsh winters).
It therefore seemed that the
relationship between life on Earth
and Earth itself was very close.
Now of course, religious people
responded to this by claiming that
such feast and famine was all part
of God's plan (or perhaps, in some
cases, God's punishment), but
science began to wonder just how
close the link was – especially as
this 'plan' seemed to lead to a quite nasty fight for existence in such times.
Could the apparent extinction of things which had once roamed the Earth be
put down to changes in food supply or some climatic event?

◆ *A shrinking world*: The UK in the 1800s was a powerful nation. Its ships sailed all
over the world and tales of these new places came filtering back home. Sailors
not only described strange new creatures but often came back with detailed
drawings of them; in some cases, stuffed versions of one or the bones of another.
The diversity of life came to be understood as something quite staggering and
very varied across the world. Why, some questioned, did God seem to make so
many different living things and seem to make only some things for some places
and not others – not to mention one popular question which asked why God
seemed to be so keen on beetles and insects as they were just so many of them!

What is the Origin of Human Life: Human Life
Emerged as a Result of the Process of Evolution?

CHAPTER 9

Again, some scientists wondered if the amazing diversity of life on Earth suggested relationships and development from common ancestors… Which of course religious people argued was quite in keeping with the idea of a creator God.

◆ *Embryology*: Advances in medicine, surgery and anatomy in Darwin's day meant that the developing embryos of a number of living things – including humans – were being studied for the first time. It was noted that the embryos of completely different species were remarkably similar at points – why would this be? For example, the early human embryo has gills and a long tail and looks very similar to the embryos of other species. What might account for these similarities other than some kind of close relationship between species?

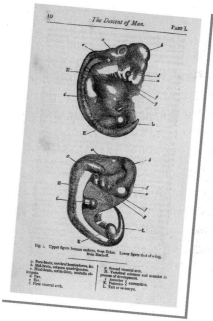

So, there was a lot for young Darwin to draw upon when he eventually got round to doing any scientific research of his own. However, Darwin was not the best student. He found studying medicine at Edinburgh very boring, so he left it to study for the priesthood at Cambridge. However, here too he found he wasn't all that interested, preferring to go out shooting and gambling and to do things which were nothing at all to do with studying. Through friendships he made, he started to develop further an interest he'd had for some time – that of a love of the natural world. So, he was pretty excited when he was invited to join a voyage around the world on HMS Beagle. This ship would travel the world making scientific and botanical observations and young Darwin was recommended for the job. He took it, and so begins his pulling together of all these diverse ideas into one theory, namely, the evolution of life on Earth through the process of natural selection.

CHAPTER 9

What is the Origin of Human Life: Human Life Emerged
as a Result of the Process of Evolution?

Talk Point

33

*The evidence for evolution so far is **circumstantial**...*
What does this mean? (revise Area 1)

Darwin's Voyage on HMS Beagle

Talk about some cruise! Darwin joined HMS Beagle as a gentleman companion to
the ship's captain, Robert FitzRoy. He was a skilled **naturalist** by this time – some
say the best one in the country – but that wasn't his job. However, he did get
special privileges on board ship, including the right to the best choice of specimens.
The man who was the ship's naturalist was so fed up with this that he left the ship
on its arrival in South America. Darwin then became the ship's naturalist. His job
now was to record and, where possible, collect animals, plants and all manner of
living things as the ship travelled around the world – and travel it did. Setting off
from the UK it travelled south, across the Atlantic, around the South American
continent, across the Pacific, round the southern coast of Australia, across the Indian
Ocean, round the southern tip of the African continent, back across to South
America and then back home to the UK.

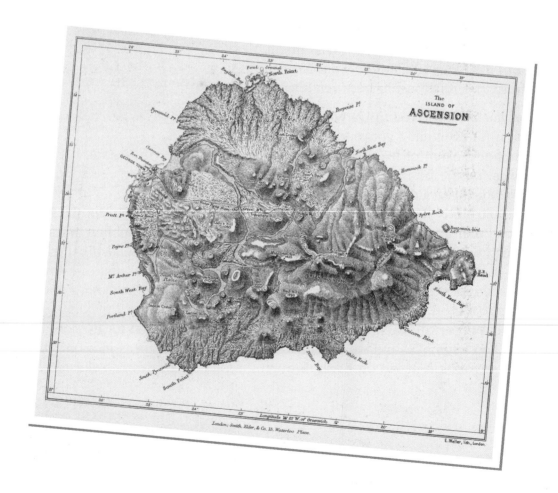

What is the Origin of Human Life: Human Life
Emerged as a Result of the Process of Evolution?

CHAPTER 9

This voyage lasted from 1831–1836 and meant that Darwin visited a staggering variety of **natural habitats** across the world, from coral reefs and the Pampas plains of South America to isolated volcanic islands. Darwin would occasionally leave the ship to travel cross-country for a while, **observing**, **recording** and **collecting** as he went. In Darwin's day, naturalists were quite happy to kill and stuff specimens and Darwin was apparently quite good at both. He also dissected other specimens and wrote up what he found. Darwin was also a keen geologist and made many records of the rocks and fossils he found. In fact, quite a lot of his published works were not on biology at all but geology. Overall, the voyage meant that Darwin's records and evidence were quite spectacularly wide and varied. All the while, he was thinking carefully about his growing feeling that the way life on Earth originated and developed was not the same as the account given in the Bible. What he experienced as he travelled the world only made this feeling stronger and the evidence seemed to support his ideas more and more. So, what evidence for his theory did he find on his grand cruise?

◆ *Fossil records:* Throughout his travels, Darwin collected rocks and **fossils**. He knew now that the Earth's natural history could be 'read' from its rocks and fossils and that these gave a historical account of the changes in life as the Earth grew older. He noticed startling similarities between fossilised life forms and living things. They weren't always exactly the same but had such similarities that they suggested a relationship of some kind. The ancient life forms bore such a resemblance to the current ones that there could only be some kind of link between them. This link was more than the simple idea that these were long-dead versions of current life forms, exactly then as they are now, there being a difference between them which suggested that they were related, but that there had been development and change from then until now.

◆ *Geographical biodiversity:* Darwin noted on his travels both wide **variation** between the life forms of certain places and some linkage too. Why, he wondered, were the life forms in South America so different from the life forms in Africa? If they had all been created at the start of life on Earth then why was there this **geographical variation** now? He was developing a realisation that geographical **isolation** had had an effect on the way that life developed in one place or other and therefore on the way that life developed generally. Darwin also noted this variation in humans – as he travelled the world he noted the differences in skin colour and facial features and body types and so on. Again, he was wondering, why there was such an amazing variety even within one species. Added to this was Darwin's discovery that living species showed variations across geographical areas – variations that had become so great that the

CHAPTER 9

What is the Origin of Human Life: Human Life Emerged
as a Result of the Process of Evolution?

creatures in question were no longer able to **interbreed**. It seemed to Darwin that the explanation must be that the species changed for some reason both with time and with geography, and changed so much that the species became quite different. Darwin came to think of it all as like a family tree, but one where some species were linked to others and developed from them or from a common ancestor, developed through time in different ways for reasons as yet unclear. These reasons were to become clear following Darwin's findings on the **Galapagos Islands**.

◆ *The Galapagos:* These are isolated volcanic islands off the coast of South America. They are extremely remote and food supply and environmental conditions vary across the small islands which make up this island group. Here Darwin found variations in types of life form between the small islands. For example, various islands had tortoises, but on each island there was a slight variation in the tortoise; some had high ridges in their shell such as those from Hood Island – 'like a Spanish saddle', said Darwin, allowing them to reach their necks up for food which was higher up off the ground. Others did not and these were found on islands where the food supply was ground-based. Darwin concluded that the variety of tortoises was related to the food supply available to them and that somehow each species had developed through time to fit more closely with its surroundings. In other words, over time it had **adapted** to the environment in which it lived. This advantageous adaptation had been passed onto offspring who demonstrated the same advantageous adaptation. Darwin referred to this as the **transmutation** of species.

Source 41

Darwin in His Own Words

It is interesting to contemplate an entangled bank, clothed with plants of many kinds, with birds singing on the bushes, with various insects flitting about, and with worms crawling through the damp Earth, and to reflect that these elaborately constructed forms, so different from each other, and dependant on each other in so complex a manner, have all been produced by laws acting around us. These laws, taken in the largest sense, being Growth and Reproduction; Inheritance which is almost implied by reproduction; Variability from the indirect and direct action of the external conditions of life, and from use and disuse... Whilst this planet has gone cycling on according to the fixed law of gravity, from so simple a beginning endless forms most beautiful and most wonderful have been, and are being, evolved.

Comment: Darwin's theory was always filled with a boyish excitement and wonder about the natural world around him. Here, he uses the variety of nature in a grassy riverbank – probably close to his home in Kent – to illustrate the theory of evolution.

Charles Darwin, On the Origin of Species in Charles Darwin: Evolutionary writings; James A. Secord (Ed) Oxford 2008 p210–211

What is the Origin of Human Life: Human Life
Emerged as a Result of the Process of Evolution?

CHAPTER 9

What Next?

For the next three years after his return from his travels, Darwin lived alone in London and worked on writing up his travels and the scientific findings he made on them. In 1839 he married his cousin, Emma Wedgwood and started a family soon afterwards. However, Darwin's health was not good at this time and soon enough he, Emma and his family moved out to a house in the quiet countryside. For the rest of his life, Darwin battled with ill-health, while continuing to work from home on his various scientific publications – mostly on the geological aspects of his *Beagle* journey, but also covering coral reefs and many other aspects of natural science. Throughout this period, Darwin's theory of evolution through natural selection was gaining strength as he linked his findings to the practice of selective breeding and many other findings of the day. However, Darwin was troubled. He realised that his theory would go against the teachings of the Church – which was very powerful in its day. Emma was also a very devout Christian and Darwin outwardly kept up his own religious life – up to a point. Some argue that his fretting over the implications of his theory contributed to his ill-health, and his worry about the reactions to his theory meant that he kept the theory from publication for many years. Darwin was not a lover of controversy and really didn't want all the attention he knew his theory would bring. However, another scientist, Alfred Russel Wallace, was independently reaching similar conclusions to Darwin and looked as if he might publish first; so Darwin and Wallace worked together and presented papers to the Linnaean Society in 1858. In 1859, a whole twenty years after his return from his voyage, he published his theory, *On the Origin of Species by Means of Natural Selection*. As he expected, great controversy did follow and remains to this day. In 1882, Darwin died and was buried, alongside the great and the good of British society, in Westminster Abbey.

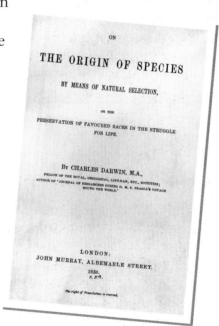

The Simple Guide to Darwin's Theory

So what did Darwin's theory really come down to? In short, like all good science, it was gloriously simple:

◆ A living thing depends upon its **environment** to survive, and it can only survive if it fits in to the environment in which it lives.

◆ Fitting in depends, for example, on a close relationship between the living thing's biology, the food source upon which it depends and the climate in which it lives. For example living in a cold climate requires a layer of insulating fat or a good outer coating of heat-trapping fur. Living where the food source is high off the ground requires the ability to reach the required height.

CHAPTER 9

What is the Origin of Human Life: Human Life Emerged as a Result of the Process of Evolution?

◆ The living things which were suited (or **adapted**) to their living conditions survived, and those which weren't, didn't.

◆ These adaptations developed through time as each generation passed on to the following generation the adaptation which increased their likelihood of survival.

◆ Just as breeders select the features they want in a species and breed only from that to pass the required features on to offspring, so **nature selects** those species which develop the necessary features to live in any particular environment.

◆ If the environment changes (gradually or rapidly), then only those who are adapted to the change survive to reproduce and pass on their survival advantages to their offspring.

This is called evolution through natural selection.

Talk Point

What problems do you think Darwin's theory might present for Christians?

34

Simple Section Summary

◆ **Charles Darwin came up with the Theory of Evolution by Natural Selection.**

◆ **He drew upon previous theories in geology, biology, breeding of livestock and population theories.**

◆ **He took part in a round the world trip on HMS Beagle where he gathered lots of his evidence for his theory, in particular:**
  - **Fossil evidence which showed changes in species with time.**
  - **Geographical biodiversity which showed that different kinds of life seemed linked to different places.**

◆ **Darwin also carried out many different kinds of experiments on many different kinds of life forms back in his home in Kent.**

◆ **Darwin published his theory 20 years after his voyage on the Beagle.**

◆ **His theory argues that just as breeders select the features they want in an animal or plant by breeding (or selecting) only those which show the feature they are after, nature also does the same.**

◆ **So, in any given environment, one species is likely to survive better than another. This selection by nature of the best suited life form in a particular location (or environmental condition) is called evolution.**

◆ **Therefore the species alive today (including humans) are those which have adapted best to the conditions of life as it is now. If conditions change then these things will have to adapt again or they will die out.**

What is the Origin of Human Life: Human Life
Emerged as a Result of the Process of Evolution?

CHAPTER 9

Some Problems for Darwin

Apart from the worry about what the theory might mean for religious belief and the controversy which would (and did) follow, Darwin probably held back his theory because there were some unresolved issues with it. For example, one of the major issues was that he could not **demonstrate** the process of evolution by natural selection, he could only **infer** it from the evidence he had. Therefore the theory was based on **circumstantial** evidence rather than being demonstrated **empirically**. For each of his scientific claims, there were religious responses which seemed to give a satisfactory religious response to the Darwinian proposal. There were also scientists who disagreed with him about his interpretation of the evidence or his theory about the mechanisms of evolution.

Also, there was one particular area of difficulty with his theory – the mechanism of evolution itself. It was well-known that qualities you develop in your life are not necessarily passed on to your offspring. For example, let's say that you spend your life sculpting your body into a muscular physique. You don't then have children who are born with huge muscles. In other words, characteristics and qualities which are developed during your lifetime are not passed on to your offspring. So if a living thing has adapted to its environment, how was that adaptation passed on to its offspring? This mechanism was not known in Darwin's day, and in fact, it wasn't until the discovery of **DNA** in the 1950s that the mechanism of evolution by natural selection was finally revealed.

DNA: The Building Block of Life

All living things are replicated according to the 'plan' written in our **DNA**. DNA, or deoxyribonucleic acid, is a spiral which contains the nucleic acids adenine, guanine, cytosine and thiamine. These **base pairs** match up in unique combinations of **genes**. The human genome has around three thousand million nucleotide bases and it is these which set the pattern for you, me and every living thing on the planet. Every feature of your physical self is based on your DNA codes and it may well be that many of your behaviours are also related to your DNA (the **nature-nurture** debate). Generally speaking, this DNA is passed on to your offspring as a combination of the DNA of the male and female of the species which reproduce through various methods of sexual reproduction. Now, every now and again genes **mutate**. This **mutation** produces a change in the offspring from the parent organism. Most often, this mutation doesn't give you any advantage – in fact it can be harmful and actually lead to the destruction of the organism. However, if this mutation leads to something which makes you better suited to your environment,

CHAPTER 9

What is the Origin of Human Life: Human Life Emerged as a Result of the Process of Evolution?

then it will lead to you being more likely to survive, and more likely to pass this beneficial (or **adaptive**) mutation to your offspring: so you evolve.

For example, let's imagine that there is a genetic **mutation** which leads to your child being able to breathe underwater for unusually long periods of time. This could lead to them becoming highly successful divers or underwater explorers. Their own children are born with the same adaptive gene which, through time, enables them and their descendants to choose to live underwater. Now let's say that some environmental disaster leads to all the land on Earth becoming uninhabitable – the people most likely to survive will be those who can take to the seas and live there... the descendants of your water-breathing child. That's evolution in action. From a random mutation we end up with a planet where all the human inhabitants have evolved to live underwater, breathing through their gills like fish – the air-breathing humans have died out and only the water-breathing ones remain. Now that's all greatly simplified but essentially that's the process. If DNA confers an advantage in a particular environment then it increases the likelihood that you and your offspring and your descendants will increase in number because of the beneficial adaptation the DNA mutation has brought.

It's important to remember that modern evolutionary theory proposes that this process is 'blind'. There is no guiding hand behind it and it is all the random changes brought about by nature which does not 'foresee' or 'plan' any changes – they just happen. For Darwinians, this blind set of chance events leading to the origin and development of life on Earth is a natural process which has nothing to do with plan or purpose, just the random interaction between DNA and the environment. Of course for others, this apparent purposelessness is a problem because it makes humans just another form of life and it suggests that there is no need for a creator. Darwinians argue that there is no need for any divine guiding hand – nature does it all, and as for humans being 'just another' form of life that doesn't need to lead to any downgrading of the value of human life – but more of that later.

The Full Implications of Evolutionary Theory

Darwinian evolutionary theory and the variations of it since Darwin's own writings agree on two main features which are important for the course you are studying:

Evolution as the Origin and Development of Life on Earth

Life on Earth began randomly and developed '**blindly**' according to the principles of evolution by natural selection. Genetic information conferred **advantages** or **disadvantages** linked to **random mutations** of DNA. If these mutations led to the organism being better suited to the environment in which it lived it survived and multiplied; if not, it died out. This explains the great extinctions of life throughout Earth's history; according to the theory, the life forms which were not suited to the environmental changes died out and those which were survived. For example, in the early history of the Earth, the gas oxygen came to be released into the atmosphere.

What is the Origin of Human Life: Human Life
Emerged as a Result of the Process of Evolution?

CHAPTER 9

This gas was toxic to some life forms, but useful to others. The life forms for whom the gas was useful survived and increased in number, the ones who weren't suited to this new oxygen-rich atmosphere died out. The early Earth was a complex mixture of materials. These materials evolved over a long period of time, always responding and adapting to changes in the environment and with time, life as we know it had become rich and stunning in its variety – filling every available niche in the environment. Modern supporters of Darwinian evolution argue that the first life forms on Earth were simple single celled organisms which had come around through a process whereby inorganic material became organic material. This remains one of the greatest areas of controversy between those who support evolution and those who do not.

Source 42

How the Inorganic became Organic

We do not know what chemical raw materials were abundant on Earth before the coming of life, but among the plausible possibilities are water, carbon dioxide, methane and ammonia: all simple compounds... Chemists have tried to imitate the chemical conditions of the young Earth. They have put these simple substances in a flask and supplied a source of energy such as ultraviolet light or electric sparks – artificial simulation of primordial lightning. After a few weeks of this something interesting is usually found inside the flask: a weak brown soup containing a large number of molecules more complex than the ones originally put in. In particular, amino acids have been found – the building blocks of proteins, one of the two great classes of biological molecules... More recently, laboratory simulations of the conditions of Earth before the coming of life have yielded organic substances called purines and pyramidines. These are the building blocks of the genetic molecule, DNA itself.

Comment: Dawkins suggests that life on Earth began as a chemical change from inorganic to organic. This produces biological molecules, which he refers to as the replicators. These free cells drifted around in a primordial soup, eventually coming together to form simple organisms, and eventually, through natural selection, forming the vast array of life forms we know today. Dawkins concludes that these replicators now 'go by the name of genes, and we are their survival machines'.

Richard Dawkins: The Selfish Gene: Oxford 1989 p14

CHAPTER 9

What is the Origin of Human Life: Human Life Emerged as a Result of the Process of Evolution?

So, life developed on Earth in a **primordial soup** (or sludge of chemicals) somehow, organic material developed and thrived. Throughout the many millions of years of life on Earth, this organic material changed and developed through natural selection to fit itself to be able to live according to the variety of climates and geographical regions on Earth. Occasionally, major events led to massive changes in the conditions for life on Earth. Those organisms suited to the changes survived, and those who did not died out. This accounts, for example, for the demise of the dinosaurs: according to evolutionary theory they were undisputed masters of the planet for far longer than humans have been around. However, it is suggested that a rapid change in climate (either the result of a meteor strike or the work of a super volcano) changed conditions so much that they were no longer favourable for the existence of such creatures and they died out, being replaced by creatures more suited to the new conditions. Living things developed in complexity, all the while fitting in closely to the environment in which they lived, including one species which began to alter its environment in significant ways so as to fit in all over the planet – us.

Source 43

Human Evolution

… we must acknowledge, as it seems to me, that man with all his noble qualities, with sympathy which feels for the most debased, with benevolence which extends not only to other men but to the humblest living creature, with his god-like intellect which has penetrated into the movements and constitution of the solar system – with all these exalted powers – Man still bears in his bodily frame the indelible stamp of his lowly origin.

What is the Origin of Human Life: Human Life
Emerged as a Result of the Process of Evolution?

CHAPTER 9

Comment: Darwin starts this book off (published in 1871, twelve years after the publication of the Origin of Species) by pointing out that although he had collected much evidence about human evolution he was 'determined not to publish' as he thought he would 'thus only add to the prejudices against my views'. Throughout the book he argues for and suggests evidence that human evolution through natural selection follows exactly the same patterns as that of all other living things.

Charles Darwin, The Descent of Man in Charles Darwin: Evolutionary writings;
James A. Secord (Ed) Oxford 2008 p333

Evolution as the Origin and Development of Human Life on Earth

The same random processes of genetic mutation and adaptation which apply to all living things obviously must apply to humans. For some, this was one of the most troubling aspects of evolutionary theory – particularly as humans were seen to be (and still are) something 'special' above and beyond animal life forms. If evolution is true, then humans are just one of the branches of primate development, sharing a common ancestry with other primates. Humans therefore are really just **hairless apes** – primates with brains which have evolved in such a way as to make us able to do the things which we can but other primates can't (like read this book for instance).

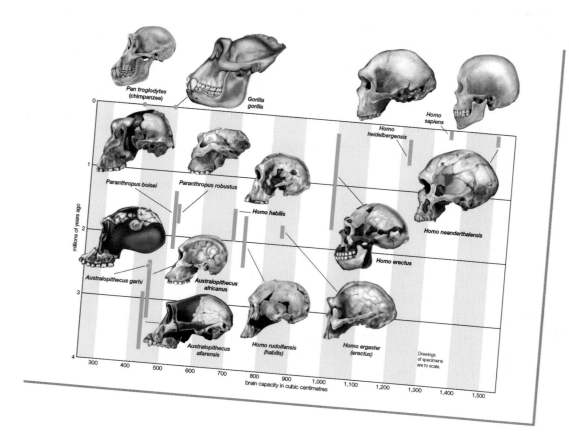

CHAPTER 9

What is the Origin of Human Life: Human Life Emerged
as a Result of the Process of Evolution?

We walk upright and communicate verbally. We use complex technology to overcome our natural limitations (for example we can fly around the world in aeroplanes), we ensure our continued survival through the application of our intelligence – though some say we also threaten our continued survival with that same intelligence.

However, in terms of our behaviour and our basic biology we are not very different from our closest primate cousins – and we share many other features with many other living things For example, our hearts beat faster when we are threatened and so does the heart of a goldfish: we try to attract mates by presenting ourselves prettily to the world – so does a peacock. All of this means that the same blind forces of evolution by natural selection apply just the same way for us as they do for all other forms of life on Earth.

For Darwinians, this closeness to other living things is not in any way something to be ashamed of or something which downgrades us as living things. It is simply a fact of life. Evolution is a blind mechanism of change and adaptation to change. It is simply who we are.

Source 44

Humans and Other Life Forms

We humans look rather different than a tree. Without a doubt we perceive the world differently than a tree does. But down deep, at the molecular heart of life, the trees and we are essentially identical. We both use nucleic acids for heredity; we both use proteins as enzymes to control the chemistry of our cells. Most significantly we both use precisely the same code book for translating nucleic acid information into protein information, as do virtually all the other creatures on the planet. The usual explanation of this molecular unity is that we are, all of us – trees and people, angler fish and slime moulds and paramecia – descended from a single and common instance of the origin of life in the early history of our planet.

Comment: All life on Earth is linked by a common process and a common history.

Carl Sagan: Cosmos; Futura 1980 p52

What is the Origin of Human Life: Human Life
Emerged as a Result of the Process of Evolution?

CHAPTER 9

Simple Section Summary

◆ Much of Darwin's theory was based on circumstantial evidence and not evidence directly demonstrated, for example, Darwin didn't know how changes in species were caused or passed on to offspring.

◆ This was all solved by the discovery of DNA in the 1950s.

◆ DNA randomly mutates and where this mutation confers an advantage in a particular environment the living thing is more likely to survive and reproduce.

◆ Therefore DNA is the major driving force behind evolution.

◆ DNA mutation and therefore natural selection is a 'blind' process which does not need the hand of a creator God behind it.

◆ Scientific materialists argue that life on Earth began in a primordial soup where inorganic elements somehow went through a process which made them organic. These then evolved over a very long period of time into the variety of life forms we have on Earth today.

◆ Humans too evolved through the same route sharing common ancestors with other primate species.

◆ This makes human life just another life form, adapted to the current environment through the same processes which apply to all other living life forms.

Strengths and Limitations of Darwinian Evolutionary Theory

Strengths	Limitations
• Darwin's Theory was meticulously researched and linked a variety of scientific disciplines together from Biology to Geology	• Much of Darwin's theory is circumstantial and based on inference as opposed to empirical evidence. This leaves it open to various interpretations
• Provides a working explanation of observable realities such as the biodiversity present on Earth and the apparent similarities between species, as well as accounting for extinctions and other major changes to life on Earth throughout Earth's history	• There are 'gaps' in the theory which remain unfilled to this day – for example in the incomplete fossil record which does not yet show intermediate species (or missing links) and so questions the gradual evolution of life. Also, the intermediate stages imply that very complex life forms had phases where their complexity was reduced to something less complex. Some living things only 'work' as complete systems – intermediary systems would not work at all

CHAPTER 9

What is the Origin of Human Life: Human Life Emerged
as a Result of the Process of Evolution?

Strengths	Limitations
• Supported by many recent developments in various scientific disciplines, for example in the discovery of DNA	• Perhaps does not suggest any meaningful answers to the question of the purpose of meaning of life
• Suggests that in the process being neutral or 'blind' there is no need for a creator who would also require an explanation for his origin	

Activities

Knowledge, Understanding, Analysis and Evaluation

1 In what different ways did Darwin come up with his theories?

2 Take two of the background ideas which Darwin would have been aware of and explain in your own words how they might challenge the idea of a creation as in Genesis.

3 How did Darwin end up on board *HMS Beagle* – and what did he do on the journey?

4 Explain how Darwin's interests in geology helped him to arrive at his evolutionary theory.

5 What did Darwin notice about people and animals as he travelled around the world and how did this contribute to his ideas about evolution?

6 In what ways were Darwin's discoveries in the Galapagos Islands particularly important for evolutionary theory?

7 Why do you think it took Darwin twenty years before he published *On the Origin of Species*?

8 Where was Darwin buried and why might this seem odd to some people?

9 Much of Darwin's evidence was circumstantial. Why is this a possible problem?

10 How did the discovery of DNA in the 1950s help Darwin's theories?

11 Explain what is meant by adaptation in evolutionary theory.

12 Describe what evolutionary theory implies about how life on Earth developed.

13 Why is the leap from inorganic material to organic material important in this debate and how does Richard Dawkins explain it?

14 How might evolutionary theory explain the extinction of the dinosaurs?

15 How does evolutionary theory link to the origin and development of human life?

16 Why might some people feel that making evolution apply to humans is a particular issue?

17 Evolution suggests that life on Earth originated and developed as a result of the chance workings of nature. Why might a religious person feel uncomfortable about this?

What is the Origin of Human Life: Human Life
Emerged as a Result of the Process of Evolution?

CHAPTER 9

Active Learning

1 Design an information poster about the evidence available to Darwin before he published his *On the Origin of Species*.

2 Design a cartoon strip about the voyage of the *Beagle*. Alternatively, you could create a PowerPoint display about this or a written travelogue detailing the places visited and the things discovered. You'll need to do some additional research to carry out this task successfully.

3 Create a short report on Darwin's findings on the Galapagos. You could do this in the form of a TV news item or a natural history-type programme. You could use ICT as well as video materials in this task.

4 Create a piece of artwork simply entitled 'Darwin'.

5 Imagine that you could write a letter to Darwin, as he lived in his home in Kent following his marriage, voyage on the *Beagle* and before he published *On the Origin of Species*. What questions would you ask him?

6 Design an information leaflet: 'An A-Z of Evolution by Natural Selection'. E.g. 'A is for Armadillo, a creature which exists only in some places of the world. This shows that life develops rather than was created at the beginning as it is now.'

7 Find out about the development of human life according to evolutionary theory, such as the development of human from ape through Cro-Magnon, Australopithecus and so on. Present your findings in whatever way you choose.

8 Discuss in class: what are the similarities and differences between humans and other primates in terms of our behaviour and appearance etc. You may like to discuss this with science teachers or a psychology teacher if you have one.

Unit Assessment Question

Higher:
Describe what is meant by the theory of evolution.　　**KU10**

Intermediate 2:
Why might evolutionary theory challenge religious belief?　　**AE4**

Intermediate 1:
Describe one piece of evidence which supports evolutionary theory.　　**KU2**

Sample Exam Question

Higher:
'Darwin's theory of evolution is based only on circumstantial evidence so it can be challenged.' How might a supporter of evolutionary theory respond to this statement?　　**AE8**

Intermediate 2:
Describe ONE piece of evidence Darwin used to support his evolutionary theory.　　**KU4**

Intermediate 1:
What did Charles Darwin mean by 'the transmutation of genes'?　　**KU4**

CHAPTER 9

What is the Origin of Human Life: Human Life Emerged as a Result of the Process of Evolution?

Homework

A famous debate took place between T.H Huxley, a supporter of Darwin, and Bishop Wilberforce, a Christian opponent of Darwinism. Carry out an internet search about this event and write up a report of your findings.

Personal Reflection

If Darwin's evolutionary theory is right, does that make human life more or less important or does it have no effect at all on the value of a human?

What is the Origin of Human Life: Are the Views of Science and Religion Compatible?

Sharon and Karen are two London girls who are visiting Scotland as part of the Homecoming celebrations. Actually they're visiting their cousins Rab and Donnie who, as ever, are playing the welcoming hosts by heading off to the nearest football match – which happens to be Sunday league stuff, but we're in a credit crunch after all. Sharon and Karen are sitting on the sofa with a slab of cheesecake and two mugs of hot chocolate, and have just been watching a David Attenborough TV programme on Darwin and evolution. They told the boys that they'd be watching some chick flick or other – well they know that Rab and Donnie aren't the brightest lads in the world and they don't want to remind them of that. As Sharon and Karen often do, they get into a really deep discussion... this time about the relationship between creation and evolution...

Sharon: So, God or Darwin, what do you fink?

Karen: Darwin every time innit?

Sharon: Whoa, slow down there girl, does it 'ave to be one or the other?

Karen: Na, prob'ly not. You could 'ave an interestin' synthesis of both, couldn't ya?

Sharon: Yeah – maybe the Good Book is smarter than we fink it is. Maybe we just ain't reading it right. Granted that some of the language it uses is a bit antiquated and therefore suggests the need for linguistic redaction and syntactical analysis, still don't mean it's wrong eh?

CHAPTER 10

What is the Origin of Human Life: Are the Views of Science and Religion Compatible?

Karen: Na – maybe it's just metaphor and allegory at a suitable level for the cognitive developmental stage of its uncivilised readers – the same people that was slaughtering goats and painting things in their blood. No point in the Big Bloke in the sky jottin' down the stuff about irreducible complexity innit?

Sharon: I know what ya mean. It does kinda look like some steps in Darwin's evolutionary theory are just too big eh? I mean, how'd it get from no wings to full wings with so many pointless steps in between. Don't make a whole lot of sense.

Karen: Too right, I mean what use would half an eye be?

Sharon: Mind you, half an eye's better than no eye at all I guess.

Karen: Yeah, half an eye up here might still save us from some of our cousins' over-friendly mates now and again.

Sharon: Know what ya mean… some of Rab and Donnie's fellow Neanderthals could be solid proof that evolution ain't made its way north of Luton yet.

Karen: Or that the Creator's got a wicked sense of humour.

Sharon: Nothin' funny about some of them – 'specially that one with the plate in 'is 'ead.

Karen: Yeugh… don't even go there girl. Anyway what about those gaps in the fossil record. They have to call Darwin's stuff into question don't ya agree?

Sharon: Well yeah – Darwin 'imself agreed that the lack of transitional forms in the fossil record was a pretty hefty challenge to his theory.

Karen: What about Archaeopteryx or Acanthostega – they're reasonable candidates for the missing links in the fossil record, no?

Sharon: Well maybe, but they are based on relatively inconclusive morphological judgments which don't take the required huge changes in gene coding into account.

Karen: Good point girl. So leaving aside punctuated equilibrium as a possibility, it looks as if we'd be trying to pack far too much biological reshufflin' into too short a time-frame.

Sharon: Looks that way, besides, the chance of things just spontaneously changing is well outside statistical probability innit? I mean, when we were playin' scrabble last night with Rab and Donnie.

Karen: 'Ha!' Says Rab, "'Squirtle' That's me done". I don't fink so.

Sharon: Too true, and he thought he could find it on wikipedia. Anyway, what do you think would be the chances of pulling at random out of the bag the word Hamburgers?

Karen: One in a million?

What is the Origin of Human Life: Are the Views of
Science and Religion Compatible?

CHAPTER 10

Sharon: Way more – in fact, you'd have to take six letters randomly out of the bag 141 million million[1] times to have a chance.

Karen: Some odds girl. Mind you, nature's had a few million years to do its stuff ain't it? I mean, it might just 'ave managed to randomly put together life as we know it through random chance mutations and adaptations given the vast timescales available to it.

Sharon: Prob'ly. Maybe we should just accept fings in faith then – just know that we're never really gonna know. After all, doesn't change our life much whether it was creation or evolution does it. I mean, we're still gonna be who we are and do what we do ain't we.

Karen: Poss'bly true, but then again maybe not. Maybe whether we're here because of the blind chance of nature or the purposeful action of a creator God really does make a difference.

Sharon: Yeah, see what ya mean...

[1]Source: Intelligent Design: The Scientific Alternative to Evolution: WS Harris & JH Calvert; National Catholic Bioethics Quarterly 2003 p544

Talk Point   35

Do you think life has a purpose?

Good Things Come in Threes

So, just like the debate over the origin of the Universe, there are three ways of responding to the issue of the origins of human life. This debate perhaps has added spice because it relates to humankind, and so has implications for our own lives and for the **meaning** and **purpose** of our lives. According to the Bible, humans were created as special beings, the pinnacle of creation – God's chosen ones. We were given '**Dominion**' over all other life and were the subjects of a special relationship with God. Now, if evolution is true and applies in the same way to humans as to every other life form then that might call into question our status as a special creation, as well as the purpose of creation and the role of God and so on. In fact, if human life is the result of chance mutations throughout the Earth's history, then that perhaps calls into question the very principles of the Christian faith (and perhaps all religion). So, this question is crucially about who we are and what our life is for. For some, creation and evolution are complete opposites and reach completely different conclusions about the nature and purpose of human life. For others of course, there are common areas between the two and a way to live with both.

CHAPTER 10

What is the Origin of Human Life: Are the Views of
Science and Religion Compatible?

Interpretation 1: Evolutionary Theory Contradicts Revelation – Rejecting Science

The Origin of Life: Biblical Creationism

The Bible's Creation Story is Right

◆ This is a recurring theme in this whole area of debate. Creationists often rely solely on the **truth of revelation** as it appears in the Bible. Unlike the creation of the Universe in relation to the Big Bang, the detail about the creation of life on Earth, concluding with the creation of human life is clearly set out. The Bible unmistakably sets out the creation of human life as something special and as something done by God. There is no suggestion that humans bear any particular relationship to any other living thing. In fact, quite the opposite – humans are seen as a special act of creation and as being above all else in creation. There is no suggestion that Adam and Eve are anything other than the first humans, and no indication at all that they are anything different to humans as they exist today. They seem to walk, talk and behave very much as humans do now (including feeling guilty, shy and so on). They are created 'in God's image' and, whatever this actually means, it is clear that this is something special and which applies only to humans. They are created for a purpose – which is to be 'in charge' of the creation which God has made, and to form a relationship with God which no other living thing seems to be able to do quite like humans. For Creationists, human life is special and its origin is clearly set out in the Bible.

◆ Accepting that the Bible story is true is an act of **faith**, unrelated to any scientific evidence supporting or challenging it. Picking and choosing which Bible texts to believe and which ones to set aside is, for the **literalist**, a dangerous activity. How could anyone decide which parts of the Bible are to be interpreted as literally true and which parts are to be understood as symbolically true (or not true at all)? Literalists believe that if it is in the Bible, it is there for a reason – we don't need to understand the reason, we just need to accept that there is one. Remember, literalists think that the Bible is divinely inspired by God – so why would he allow something to be present in the Bible if it wasn't true? That would make no sense at all. Besides, literalists often argue, picking and choosing which bits of the Bible to believe or ignore is a route to disbelief. Humans can't make such decisions – simply trust and believe.

◆ The Bible's account of the creation of human life is supported by Biblical texts all through the Bible. For the prophets, Paul and Jesus himself, Adam and Eve are thought to be real people as well as the first people. The literal truth of this story is, literalists claim, supported all through the Bible. If it had simply been a simple tale for simple folk then why would God not have updated it as he inspired the writers of biblical materials written long after the Genesis story? Remember too, that the written form of Genesis is probably based on the story being passed down **orally** from one generation to another. Previous generations were very skilled at remembering the details of stories (perhaps more than we are nowadays) because this was the only way they could remember their past and

What is the Origin of Human Life: Are the Views of
Science and Religion Compatible?

CHAPTER 10

hand it on before writing developed. So, there's no reason to doubt that the story in Genesis is exactly what was passed down through the ages. Besides which, this story is perhaps the most important story there is – so those who passed it on would be careful to get it right word for word.

◆ Even those who understand the story as more **symbolic** than literal can still argue that it is true and therefore evolution is not. The story might not go into scientific detail about the mechanism of the creation of human life but why should it? Its purpose as a story is to explain *why* human life was created not *how* it was created. It gives humanity a special place in the created order as well as a special role in relation to God. It is not a textbook of biology but an explanation of what it means to be human and what rights and responsibilities that gives our species. So you can read the story and feel confident that it points to the truth of the origin of human life if not the actual literal detail of it.

So, all in all, evolutionary theory is rejected because it **contradicts literal readings of scripture**. The scriptural accounts of the creation of human life are **factual**, therefore evolution is wrong. However, scientific materialists will argue against this because it does two things:

◆ Firstly it relies on **faith** alone which means that **evidence** and **argument** is not part of the discussions because the belief rests on belief alone. This means that it becomes simply a matter of what you believe and of course belief isn't so open to scientific challenge.

◆ Secondly it uses the truth of the Bible to demonstrate… the truth of the Bible. Some religious people also find this '**circular argument**' problematic because if someone does not accept the authority or validity of the Bible then there's not much point in using the Bible alone to convince them of anything.

For these reasons, as well as many others, a new branch of Creationism has developed which goes beyond the simple argument that 'if it's in the Bible it's right' to support its view that human life (all life in fact) is not about random chance mutations leading to evolution, but that it is guided throughout by the hand of an **intelligent designer**.

Strengths and Limitations of Biblical Literalism on the Origin of Life

Strengths	Limitations
• Clear and unambiguous – if the Bible says so it's true	• Uses the truth of the Bible to prove the truth of the Bible and so is a circular argument and not open to debate with anyone who doesn't accept the Bible as true
• Suggests answers to the question of the meaning and purpose of human life even if not the biological mechanism of its origin	• Does not take into account any scientific evidence for or against the events of the creation story

CHAPTER 10

What is the Origin of Human Life: Are the Views of
Science and Religion Compatible?

The Origin of Life: Intelligent Design

Source 45

Intelligent Design

What is Intelligent Design?

Something has been intelligently designed when it is the end product of a
thoughtful process that had that product in mind. In other words, Intelligent Design
originates in a mind. The 'intelligence' in Intelligent Design is an awareness, or
consciousness, that is purposeful, that conceives of something it wants to see
actualized and directs whatever activities are necessary to achieve that end.

Comment: Supporters of Intelligent Design start with the idea that life on Earth is
created by God. However, they go beyond the Bible text to support this belief with
hard scientific evidence. Some of this is very complex indeed and beyond the
scope of this course.

Steve Renner: An Introduction to Intelligent Design at www.ideacenter.org

There are some very good websites which set out in detail the scientific arguments
which supporters of Intelligent Design use in support of the creation of life by God.
It is very important to be aware here that:

◆ Supporters of Intelligent Design are most often highly qualified scientists and who
use their understanding of science to challenge evolutionary theory according to
the **standard conventions** of scientific enquiry (observation, hypothesis,
experiment and so on). They use **scientific method** in the same way as scientific
materialists, but reach different conclusions about the origin of life on Earth.

◆ They may also refer to scientists who do not support creation of life by God,
but who question evolutionary theory. This is important to note because you
could easily think that supporters of Intelligent Design are just religious people
looking to support their own views and finding evidence to do so, but they draw
upon evidence produced by *scientists who are not aiming to suggest that creation
was carried out by God.*

The arguments and the science supporting them is complex of course, and much of
it demands an understanding of the fine details of evolutionary theory beyond what
this course and therefore this book is able to cover. However, the Intelligent Design
and Awareness Center sets out the basics of Intelligent Design in a series of articles
covering the basics 'in a nutshell'. All of these are based on the principle that the
origin and development of life on Earth cannot have happened according to the
chance mechanism suggested by Darwinian evolutionary theory and the neo-
Darwinism which followed it. The probability of life developing the way it has is just
too great to have happened by chance – even given the vast geological timescales
available in which it could have happened. This probability issue leads to the

argument that an **intelligent designer** must be behind it all.

What is the Origin of Human Life: Are the Views of
Science and Religion Compatible?

CHAPTER 10

Intelligent Design in a Nutshell

The following bullet points are based on the information found on the website of the Intelligent Design and Evolution Awareness Center (www.ideacenter.org). Each point makes a case for Intelligent Design as a response to what it regards as the flaws in Darwin's evolutionary theory. Intelligent Design works on the same principles as science. It suggests hypotheses and then tests these hypotheses out according to scientific method. It concludes that this process points to an intelligent designer.

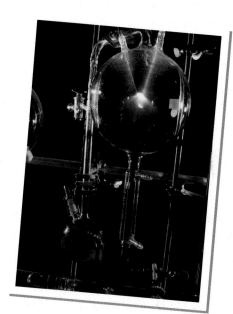

- *The origin of life*: Neo-Darwinism argues that organic matter can arise spontaneously from inorganic matter as in the 'Miller-Urey flask experiment' (See Dawkins' quote on p163). It is argued that this did not use the same gases that were present in the Earth's early atmosphere, and that the geological evidence does not support the existence of a 'primordial soup'. Besides, even if amino acids had been created in a lab flask, this doesn't automatically support the theory that they were created in the early Earth atmosphere.

- *A common family tree*: Darwinism suggests that all life is related and this can be shown through the construction of 'phylogenetic trees'. This is based on a previous assumption of common *descent* which could just as well be explained by common *design*

- *Developmental evidence*: The similarities between human embryos and the embryos of other living things are used to support Darwinian evolution. The website calls the evidence for this into question and argues that the embryos begin differently and end differently – even if there are similarities along the way. It concludes that such 'similarities' are not strong enough evidence upon which to base a whole theory.

- *Mutations*: Neo-Darwinism argues that random mutations confer advantages which result in the evolution of species. The website argues that most mutations are harmful and that even those that are beneficial do not need to lead automatically to the development of a whole new species.

- *Irreducible complexity*: Darwinian Theory suggests that evolution is a gradual process of adaptation and change. However, the website argues that such 'step by step' changes don't add up. It argues that an organism only 'works' if all the parts are present in the correct manner. For example, it argues that the 'function of a partly evolved wing is almost impossible to conceive'. It argues further that the complex designs of life on Earth did not arise from earlier less complex designs as such stages of development would have been meaningless and useless to the life forms which had developed them

CHAPTER 10

What is the Origin of Human Life: Are the Views of Science and Religion Compatible?

◆ *The fossil record*: Darwin himself pointed out that the absence of a complete fossil record challenged his theory. The website suggests that the absence of intermediate stages (missing links) between one species and its 'evolved' descendant in the fossil record brings into question the whole theory of evolution. If it were true, then the intermediate stages of developing life would have shown up in the fossil record by now.

Source 46

Intelligent Design on the Offensive

According to arch-Darwinist Richard Dawkins, Darwin made it possible to be an intellectually fulfilled atheist. Not any more. Intelligent Design is showing that systems after biological system is beyond the reach of blind purposeless material processes like the Darwinian mechanism of natural selection... This explains why Intelligent Design is so controversial: it claims to discover signs of intelligence in biological systems for which the underlying intelligence is not, and indeed cannot be, an evolved intelligence. Thus while not directly proving that God exists, Intelligent Design is far more friendly to theism than Darwinism. Intelligent Design puts the ball back in Darwinism's court.

Comment: Dembski argues that Intelligent Design is a more than credible alternative to Darwinism. He goes on in the article to outline ten questions which can be used to discuss evolution with its supporters...

William A Dembski: Ten Questions to ask your Biology Teacher about Design at www.designinference.com/documents/2004.01.Ten_Questions_ID.pdf

So the science here is complex, but supporters of Intelligent Design argue that the scientific information is there to prop up their belief that the origin of life lies in creation by God.

Strengths and Limitations of Intelligent Design on the Origin of Life

Strengths	Limitations
• Strong scientific basis for the arguments properly researched according to scientific method.	• Scientific argument is complex and demands a high level of understanding which may put it beyond the reach of ordinary people including Christian believers who are not scientifically literate.

What is the Origin of Human Life: Are the Views of
Science and Religion Compatible?

CHAPTER 10

Strengths	Limitations
• Does away with the need to use only biblical support for creation against evolution.	• Perhaps implies that the Bible's creation story is not enough.
• Tackles the possible flaws in evolutionary theory (Darwinist and neo-Darwinist versions) and suggests credible alternatives.	• Ultimately rests on the idea of belief for the existence of God. Much like Hume's criticism of the teleological argument – even if all of evolutionary theory was shown to be wrong and all the theories of Intelligent Design were shown to be right it still would not prove that God had created/designed life on Earth – nor would it prove anything about the nature of God. In fact, it simply leads to the further problem of what kind of intelligent being designed the intelligent designer and so on backwards eternally…

So Christians can reject the theories of Darwinian evolution either because they
contradict the teaching of the Bible or because there seems to be convincing
scientific evidence to reject it. Some Christians may accept the Intelligent Design
arguments and some may not, but still reject Darwinian evolutionary theory because
they consider its limitations outweigh its strengths.

Simple Section Summary

◆ Biblical literalists argue that the creation of human life in the Bible is
literally true – therefore humans did not evolve.
◆ This is based on faith and belief and therefore rejects any evidence
which contradicts it.
◆ Some Christians accept the story of human origins in the Bible as
symbolism. It is not designed as science but simply as a way to explain
what human life is for.
◆ So evolution is rejected because it contradicts scripture.
◆ Supporters of Intelligent Design argue that there is scientific evidence
supporting creation of human life by God, using (for example)
arguments based on ideas such as irreducible complexity.

Interpretation 2: Revelation Contradicts Evolutionary Theory – Rejecting Christian Belief

The Origin of Life: Evolutionary Theory – A Blind Self-Regulating System

For many scientific materialists, evolution is regarded as a fact rather than a belief. However, according to the model of the scientific method which we have explored throughout this book, perhaps we should think of it as somewhere between these two. It remains a **theory** – and it could be overturned tomorrow should convincing **contradictory evidence** be discovered and validated by the scientific community. If such evidence is found then, in line with the principles of scientific method, evolutionary theory will be replaced. Now it's true that it wouldn't be replaced overnight – it has become accepted theory within science and has a lot of weight of evidence in its favour. Also, there would probably be scientists whose whole lives had been built on evolutionary theory who wouldn't give it up easily – but eventually the scientific community would if something better came along. However, for the moment, the vast majority of scientists agree that evolutionary theory is the best bet for explaining the origin and development of life on Earth. There are scientists who disagree with it – some of whom are religious and some not – but for the moment it is the dominant theory.

One important feature of evolutionary theory for your study is this: evolution is a **blind process** of adaptation and change – it depends on nothing other than the laws of nature and the relationship between living things and their surroundings to work. For scientific materialists, evolution does away with the need for any divine being starting life off or guiding its development along the way. So, upon what do scientific materialists base their support for evolutionary theory?

The Scientific Facts and Theories Available

◆ Darwinists and neo-Darwinists know that evolutionary theory isn't perfect. There probably remain areas which still require supporting evidence and there are still probably unanswered questions surrounding the theory. However their argument is simple: evolution is the *best explanation* we *currently* have for the origin and development of life on Earth.

The Bible's Creation Story is Wrong

Now of course, many scientific materialists won't even get into this debate because they don't see it as relevant to their understanding of evolution. However, those who do might criticise the biblical account of creation on the following grounds:

◆ Biblical texts are a product of their time and place. The creation myth is simply the way one group of people (in the case of the Bible a small nomadic tribal group in the Middle East) explain their origins in story form. There are many creation myths across the world – from the epic of Gilgamesh to the Aboriginal dreamtime myth. Are they all true? Why should one myth be accepted and another

What is the Origin of Human Life: Are the Views of
Science and Religion Compatible?

CHAPTER 10

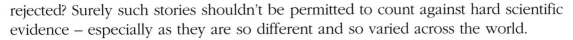

rejected? Surely such stories shouldn't be permitted to count against hard scientific evidence – especially as they are so different and so varied across the world.

◆ The Bible's creation story is regarded as literally true by some Christians and as symbolic by others. Many Christians do pick and choose which bits of the Bible to accept and which to reject. With such a lack of consistency even within Christianity, how can the story be taken seriously as a possible alternative to evolutionary theory?

◆ The story was probably passed on orally – stories passed on in this way have a habit of becoming exaggerated, as well as introducing errors as they are passed down. Also, this story belongs to what became – through human historical processes – the dominant planetary world faith (according to one way of looking at it) so the story has become the dominant creation myth. Its writers and those who uphold it therefore have a strong interest in ensuring that it is accepted.

◆ Other biblical figures do seem to have accepted the story as factually true, but what else would you expect? They lived in times and places where it was the dominant creation myth and so reflected this in their own beliefs. Also, as their own writings were organised and recorded it is likely that any such acceptance of the creation myth would have been strengthened and further set in stone. In other words their writings may have been modified so as to match up with earlier writings (for example, some Christians argue that the birth story of Jesus was edited in such a way as to strengthen the link between his birth and the messiah promised in the Old Testament).

◆ You cannot base the truth of the biblical story on the truth of the Bible. This is a circular argument and can only be accepted by someone who already accepts the Bible.

◆ Faith seems to be the key ingredient in accepting the Bible's creation story. That's fine if you are a Christian, but a scientific materialist could not accept that faith is a valid replacement for evidence produced through scientific method. A scientific materialist requires evidence and there is no evidence for the Bible's creation myth.

So scientific materialists, where they get into such debates, would respond that the Bible's creation story and the theory of evolution are completely different things. One is faith-based and one is fact-based. However, scientific materialists also have to contend with the arguments from supporters of Intelligent Design, which are claimed to be scientifically founded. How might a scientific materialist respond to the claims of **Intelligent Design**?

The Theories of Intelligent Design are Wrong

◆ *ID = God?* First off, and perhaps most challenging to the Intelligent Design argument is this: Even if every single shred of scientific evidence supported the theory of Intelligent Design and the evolutionary theory was completely rejected, it still does not need to point to the existence of the Christian God. Perhaps the Intelligent Creator was from a different species on a different planet. Perhaps it was a group of gods – like the Greek ones of Mount Olympus. Perhaps it was a God from one of the other faiths of the world – like Brahman. Perhaps it was a God completely unknown to us and perhaps he or she is a completely unlikable God. Perhaps too, it was the Christian God, but maybe he was so disgusted with Adam's disobedience that he simply disappeared and had absolutely nothing to do with life on Earth ever again. Also, Intelligent Design still does not answer the basic question about who designed the intelligent designer – it just takes the existence of God as based on faith despite all its scientific claims. It has no scientific evidence for the existence of God, only scientific theories which support the idea of an intelligent designer. But what about the actual scientific claims of Intelligent Design – can they be challenged?

- ◆ *Origins of Life*: Scientific materialists claim that the **Miller-Urey Flask** experiment did create **organic** matter from **inorganic.** It doesn't matter how much or how little, but it did. Also, it may not have created exactly the same conditions as life on the primitive Earth, but it was close enough to demonstrate the possibility that the organic can spontaneously arise from the inorganic.

- ◆ *A common family tree*: Common descent or common design is probably a matter of faith. However, the more we learn about the genetic code the more it seems that humans and primates are genetically linked rather than simply examples of God re-using and recycling ideas and body parts.

- ◆ *Developmental evidence*: Scientific materialists maintain that the similarities between the embryos of different species point to common lines of origin in our genetic past.

- ◆ *Mutations*: Whether a genetic mutation is 'advantageous' or 'harmful' is a matter of interpretation as well as of circumstances. For example, in the past having poor eyesight would have been a great disadvantage – in fact it would probably have led to an early death in the hunt. However, nowadays having poor eyesight might mean that you don't get called up to serve in the armed forces during a war (and therefore possibly having a greater chance of surviving than those with good eyesight). So bad eyesight can be an advantageous mutation as well as a harmful one depending upon the circumstances. (an argument suggested by the evolutionist John Maynard Smith).

- ◆ *Irreducible complexity*: Scientific materialists argue that the evolutionary steps from no eye to eye (for example) mean that you do not need a fully functioning eye, for it to 'work'; Richard Dawkins refers to such thinking as examples of the 'discontinuous mind' where only one or other extreme alternative is accepted. Eyes come in all shapes and forms and have developed gradually. Through random mutation, a few light-sensitive cells in the body in early life forms gave them an advantage over completely blind organisms. You could more easily avoid predators or spot something tasty to eat. This is a long way from the complex human eye but it was a step along the way. So, according to scientific materialists, more complex structures do go through simpler stages – and given the timescales available to evolutionary change – this is not beyond statistical probability.

What is the Origin of Human Life: Are the Views of
Science and Religion Compatible?

CHAPTER 10

◆ *The fossil record*: If the age of the Earth is calculated according to the genealogy of Adam, then it works out as being thousands of years old. Geological evidence contradicts this and points to an Earth much older than that. Now it is true that not all the intermediate stages of evolution show up in the fossil record and so there is an incomplete record of evolutionary change; and one which does not fully support all the elements of evolution. However, it is very risky to base opposition to evolution based on what *is not there*. Perhaps these gaps will soon be filled and then what for supporters of Intelligent Design? Fossil creation is a very specific process and perhaps we shouldn't expect there to be examples of every species at every stage of its evolutionary development. Also, fossil discovery can be a little haphazard – perhaps the intermediate stages (missing links) are out there but just haven't been discovered yet. Again, like all of these points, no matter what the fossil record does or does not support – it cannot be used to point conclusively to the actions of a creator God – and in particular the creator God Christians believe in.

Source 47

Irreducible Complexity

'What is the use of half an eye?'... as soon as we give these assumptions a moment's thought, we immediately see the fallacy. A cataract patient with the lens of her eye surgically removed can't see clear images without glasses, but she can see enough not to bump into a tree or fall over a cliff. Half a wing is →

CHAPTER 10

What is the Origin of Human Life: Are the Views of Science and Religion Compatible?

indeed not as good as a whole wing, but it is certainly better than no wing at all. Half a wing could save your life by easing your fall from a tree of a certain height. And 51% of a wing could save you if you fall from a slightly taller tree... By analogy... it is easy to imagine situations in which half an eye would save the life of an animal where 49 % would not... As I keep saying and will say again, however little we know about God, the one thing we can be sure of is that he would have to be very complex and presumably irreducibly so!

Comment: Dawkins argues that evolutionary mutations are gradual steps and that they confer step-by-step advantages. He compares this to the idea of God, suggesting that if supporters of Intelligent Design can accept that God is a complex being who had no intermediary steps then why would anything else need them?

Richard Dawkins: The God Delusion; London 2006 pp149–151

So, according to scientific materialists, evolutionary theory provides a realistic alternative to the Christian creation story – one based on evidence and all the elements of the scientific method you are now aware of. So, how is it that there are scientists who are Christians and how do some Christians manage to accept both Christian teaching and the findings of evolutionary theory?

Talk Point

Do you think science effectively responds to Intelligent Design theories?

Simple Section Summary

◆ Scientific materialists argue that the evidence in favour of evolution by natural selection is overwhelming

◆ Besides which it is the best explanation we have available – even if it is not perfect

◆ They argue that you cannot use the Bible to oppose evolution as the Bible just isn't up to the job in far too many respects

◆ Scientific materialists also reject the theories of Intelligent Design on many fronts – for example in the argument that even if every theory of Intelligent Design were shown to be completely accurate, it still is not direct evidence for the existence of a God

◆ Scientific materialists challenge all the claims of Intelligent Design as either bad science or science interpreted in a particular way – one which is already based on belief in a creator God

What is the Origin of Human Life: Are the Views of Science and Religion Compatible?

CHAPTER 10

Interpretation 3: Revelation and the Theory of Evolution Both Contribute to a Full Understanding of the Origins of Human Life

Source 48

Creation in Evolution

Science is alienating if it is approached as a self-sufficient totality which claims to say all that can be said about humanity; however, the true scientist recognises the limits to scientific method... The Christian who is already familiar with the presence of God in history can envisage biological evolution, and similarly the evolution of the Universe, as the overall way in which creation unfolds.

Comment: This entire book is written by Christians who are also scientists. The argument throughout is that evolution is the mechanism through which God created life on Earth. The back of the book comments: "they show how evolution can be read as a demonstration of the creative activity of God".

C Montenat, L Plateaux & P Roux: How to read the World: Creation in Evolution: SCM Press 1985 p13

Evolution: God's Mechanism?

The source above opens with a quote (p19) from Joel de Rosnay in *Les Origines de la Vie* which states "I believe that if we are to respect the many implications of the origin of life and to avoid reducing it to one particular area – whether science, philosophy or religion – we must consider it simultaneously from a scientific, a philosophical and a religious perspective".

De Rosnay's argument is understood by many Christians to be a way forward in the creation-evolution debate and that is to consider the two explanations for the origin and development of life as **complementary** rather than **conflicting**. In other words, evolution is to be understood as the **mechanism** through which God created life on Earth and allowed life to develop according to the laws of nature which he also set up. Therefore, the two are not opposites but simply two independent ways of looking at the same thing. How does this work?

◆ The biblical creation story is understood either as a myth or with a symbolic meaning. It exists only to explain that God created everything including humans and it contains messages about the relationship between God and his creation. It is not intended as science, nor should its simplicity be understood as counting against science – it is what it is.

CHAPTER 10

What is the Origin of Human Life: Are the Views of
Science and Religion Compatible?

◆ Of course, the Adam and Eve story could be literally true and still not count
against evolution. Perhaps the story refers to *a* first man and woman rather than
the first man and woman. The story is about two of the early humans who
represent human life and its development and special relationship with God.
This would get round the Cain's wife problem as well as allow for the possibility
that up to that point evolutionary forces had been responsible for the
development of life on Earth.

◆ The Bible story of the creation of human life isn't meant to outline scientific
principles – it has different functions. So we should not expect it to stand up
to comparison with the evidence supporting evolution – it wasn't intended for it
to do so.

◆ To argue that the closeness of humans to other primates (or any other life
forms) is something negative suggests a very poor view of God's creation.
Humans can still be special even if there is some kind of genetic relationship
with other life forms. In fact, some Christian supporters of evolution argue,
such closeness is an advantage because we're more likely to act as responsible
'stewards' of God's creation if we have a sense of being closely related to it.
Nowadays, many Christians are joining up with those who call for greater
protection for the natural world and its life forms. Some are doing so because
they understand that '**dominion**' means **responsibility** not **exploitation** (not
always the view taken by Christians throughout the history of the faith). Others
are probably doing so because science reveals more and more our closeness to
other living things and our **interdependence** with them. So evolutionary
discoveries bind us closer to our non-human neighbours rather than further away
from them – and that can only be a good thing for life on Earth.

What is the Origin of Human Life: Are the Views of
Science and Religion Compatible?

CHAPTER 10

◆ Accepting evolutionary theory also means that Christians don't have to get into complex contortions of argument to explain it away. Too many opponents of evolution perhaps rest upon the 'gaps' in the theory. However, history has shown that the '**God of the gaps**' approach is a dangerous way upon which to defend your faith. Every time a gap is 'plugged' by some new discovery, Christians would have to revise their opposition and perhaps the gap into which you can fit God gets smaller and smaller. Is this any way to propose a belief system – or is it just running scared from scientific findings?

◆ Instead, many Christians argue, accepting the mechanism of evolution as the way in which life began and developed on our planet is not something which challenges God, but something which honours him. The more detail we find out about the complexity of life and the more we find out about the way in which it developed, the more incredible its creator seems. Many Christians argue that belief in God can only be strengthened by an understanding –and acceptance – of evolutionary theory. Why should God *not* have used evolution as a way to start and develop life on Earth?

Source 49

God in Creation

Science is concerned with description, religion with encounter. Science can be viewed as learning about God by studying his creation... Christianity is a personal relationship with and personal response to the Mind behind the Universe and life. In accepting the truth of a Universe where planet Earth is moving around the sun, in appreciating some of the vast activities and events that are going on at the edge of a galaxy where there are millions of other suns with their planets and moons, the believer is moved to praise God for the greatness of this creation. The knowledge of the Big Bang and the expanding Universe, of the origin of life and it meaning may just set our minds buzzing, or it may suddenly wake us up to appreciate "The Mighty One, God the Lord!"

Comment: Brooks is a geochemist and well-qualified scientist. Throughout his book he argues that the more we uncover about nature the more it points to the actions of a creator God, and that belief in God and belief in the findings of science do not need to be contradictory.

Jim Brooks: Origins of Life: Lion 1985 p154

CHAPTER 10

What is the Origin of Human Life: Are the Views of
Science and Religion Compatible?

Evolution as Explaining the Physical Origins of Life on Earth

So Christians can accept evolution as something which does not contradict religious belief because it refers only to the **physical** dimension of life on Earth. Religious belief concerns the physical but it also concerns the **spiritual** dimension to existence. Evolutionary theory *arguably* has nothing to say about spiritual issues but, Christians would argue, religious belief does. Therefore when you put all the evidence and counter-evidence together it still cannot add up to a contradiction of religious belief because it is in a totally different sphere. This is what Gould was getting at in his NOMA concept: Religious belief and Evolutionary theory are like oil and water – they can exist side by side but don't mix. However, just as oil doesn't cancel out the properties of water and vice-versa, so too evolution does not cancel religious belief nor does belief in a creator God cancel out evolutionary theory.

Many Christians argue that one of the features about humans which makes them 'special' in creation is that they were created '**in the image of God**'. One thing this might mean is that human curiosity is matched by human intelligence. So it is inevitable that we will want to *and be able to* uncover things about the world in which we live. Perhaps one of these is evolution. Perhaps, in learning about how the Universe works we are not being arrogant, but instead, just being what God wants us to be – fully human. Perhaps, and here's an interesting thought, God created a being which – through its own endeavours – could get close to the level of understanding of nature which *he* has – and that wouldn't make mankind a rival *but a companion*. Perhaps as Francis Bacon (1561–1626) said; 'A little science estranges a man from God; a little more brings him back' Which leads nicely to the final argument in this book and so your course…

What is the Origin of Human Life: Are the Views of
Science and Religion Compatible?

CHAPTER 10

Talk Point   37

Do you think life on Earth has an ultimate goal?

What on Earth are You Doing There, Sitting Reading this Book?

There are probably many reasons for that, but you are doing it. We could spend some considerable time discussing the benefits and drawbacks of education as well as the place of RMPS in your school and so on. But here's a suggestion: You're doing this course because you're interested in life's big questions. You want to find out more about the variety of beliefs human beings have and you want to think through big meaningful questions like 'Does God exist?' and 'What is human life for?' You also want to pass an exam so you have 'qualifications' so that you can study more or get a job and so on, and maybe have children who'll do it all over again… Why? Perhaps one argument is that it is human nature to ask questions and seek answers. Perhaps it's all about our survival – the more we know and understand, the more we're likely to survive. Perhaps it's all because that's just how humans are. We're probably not going to arrive at an answer for that question (or indeed anything else) but our human nature doesn't stop us trying. Maybe of course this is the key to the whole evolution/creation/ Big Bang/God/Nature debate: the purpose and goals of human life are not to be explained only by one way of thinking, but by many ways combined.

Evolution can explain the physical origins of human life and why we have developed the way we have. Religious revelation adds to that with explanations for important questions about the **purpose and goals of life**.

The Purpose and Goals of Life

So, is this book about to explain the **meaning of life**? Well partly. For supporters of evolutionary theory there is no ultimate 'goal' of life on Earth, nor any real 'purpose' behind it. That doesn't mean that we can live life however we want though, nor does it make life meaningless. In fact, many Darwinians argue that it makes our life even more precious because we only have one and it is relatively short. Therefore we should enjoy every moment of it. Nor does it mean that evolution is about killing off the opposition in the struggle for survival (the misunderstood 'survival of the fittest' argument – a phrase which has not so far appeared in this book - and with good reason). Many opponents of evolution argue that it opens the door to selfishness and behaviours which are negative and do not lead to a better world. Of course this is debatable. Humans do bad things to each other as well as great things for each other. Human **altruism** is perhaps just as much a technique of survival as **aggression** (and altruistic behaviour is probably a much more successful long-term strategy than aggressive behaviour). Perhaps evolution has always been

CHAPTER 10

What is the Origin of Human Life: Are the Views of Science and Religion Compatible?

about being better – or being the best that we can be as a species. This doesn't mean that there's any '**consciousness**' on the part of the evolutionary process, it just does what it does.

However, in that it fits existing life forms as best it can into the current environment is really pretty neat after all. Perhaps any '**purpose**' in life under evolutionary theory comes from ensuring the survival of your genes to the next generation, and so protecting your offspring and making the world the kind of place you'd be happy for them to live in isn't a bad reason for living. Also, as far as '**meaning**' is concerned, perhaps evolutionary theory makes life more meaningful instead of less. Knowing that you have only one life and that it is the end result of many millions of

years of change and development perhaps should make you cherish it even more – for once you are gone, you're gone. So life's meaning becomes far more closely linked to the here and now, and not any less meaningful for that.

For Christians, some of these ideas could equally be accepted. Christians also believe that life has a 'purpose'. The passing on of our beliefs and values to our children is important, as is creating a world fit for them to live in. Also, living life to the full is equally important in Christian teaching. Of course, within religion there are dimensions to this which are not present in evolutionary theory. For example, Christians believe that God has a '**plan**' and an ultimate purpose for the existence of each human being and for all human life in general. Humans do not know what that plan is all about – only God does, but it should make life more meaningful rather than less, for if it is true then we are all an important part of it in one way or another. Also, for Christians, life does not end at death – a crucial difference in belief between a religious person and a non-religious one. This too however should make life all the more meaningful because the consequences of our lives do not end with our physical death but go on for all eternity. So, when all's said and done

What is the Origin of Human Life: Are the Views of
Science and Religion Compatible?

CHAPTER 10

scientific materialists and Christians agree that life **means** something and should be both cherished and enjoyed. They differ in their explanations about why this is so, but they both agree that it is. So whether you are a Christian or a scientific materialist (or some combination of the two), enjoy the life you have and make it a meaningful one.

Simple Section Summary

◆ Some people accept both evolution and creation as explanations of the origin of life on Earth.

◆ Perhaps evolution is the mechanism by which God creates and regulates life on Earth.

◆ Perhaps evolutionary theory gives answers about the physical and material dimensions of life on Earth while religion gives answers about the non-physical and spiritual dimensions to life.

◆ In short, evolution explains the physical processes of life while religion explains the meaning and purpose of life.

◆ However, both scientific materialists and Christians believe that life is valuable and should be cherished.

Activities

Knowledge, Understanding, Analysis and Evaluation

1 What is 'dominion'?

2 According to the Bible, what is the purpose of human life?

3 Why might it be a problem for a Christian to accept some parts of the Bible and reject others?

4 How might later biblical writings support the truth of the Genesis creation story?

5 Is 'believing through faith' a strong or weak argument for opposing evolution?

6 In what way might someone think that 'circular arguments' are used about the creation story by Christians?

7 What is the main argument of supporters of Intelligent Design?

8 Choose one of the 'Intelligent Design in a nutshell' arguments and explain in your own words.

9 Do supporters of evolutionary theory think it is perfect? Is this a problem?

10 Explain one way in which a scientific materialist might challenge the Bible's creation story.

11 Explain how a scientific materialist would challenge two of the claims made by supporters of Intelligent Design.

12 Explain the argument for and against 'irreducible complexity'.

CHAPTER 10

What is the Origin of Human Life: Are the Views of
Science and Religion Compatible?

13 What argument is put forward by Joel de Rosnay? What do you think about this argument?

14 Choose two of the arguments which suggest that science and religion are compatible in their explanations of the origins of life and explain them in your own words. What are your views on the arguments?

15 What is meant by the 'God of the gaps' argument and what different views are held about it?

16 Why might being 'created in the image of God' be important for human life?

17 Is it true, in your opinion, that religion explains spiritual questions and evolutionary theory physical ones?

18 What do you think of the idea of God requiring a companion?

19 In what different and similar ways do religious people and scientific materialists explain the meaning and purpose of life?

20 What do you think the meaning and purpose of life is?

Active Learning

1 Rab and Donnie return from the Sunday League football and join Karen and Sharon in their discussion. Write the script (and act it out if you're feeling brave).

2 Create (design?) an information leaflet about Intelligent Design arguments. You may present alternative points of view if you like.

3 Write a short song outlining the two viewpoints you have covered in this section. Your song should include a chorus which covers the views of those who believe that both science and religion are right. You could use a well known tune as the melody for your song.

4 Turn the information in this section (or in the book overall) into a popular game show format (e.g. 'Mastermind' or 'Who Wants to be a Millionaire?' for example).

5 Script and film a short interview with a Christian who accepts evolutionary theory.

6 Write a poem: The Meaning of Life.

7 Respond to this letter based on what you have been studying throughout this course.

Dear Sir
Why are pupils in school taught that evolution is a fact? What about the alternatives? It's about time they had their eyes opened to other possibilities…

8 Write an account of how your views have changed about any of the issues you have studied in this course. If they haven't changed, explain why and consider what you might need to know or be challenged with to change them – or are they unchangeable – if so why?

What is the Origin of Human Life: Are the Views of
Science and Religion Compatible?

CHAPTER 10

Unit Assessment Question

Higher:
'Christians can accept both evolution and creation.' Do you agree? Give reasons for your answer.   **AE8**

Intermediate 2:
*'Evolution proves there is no God.'
How might a Christian respond to this statement?*   **AE4**

Intermediate 1:
Why might a Christian disagree with evolution?   **KU4**

Sample Exam Question

Higher:
In what ways might the theory of evolution challenge a Creationist view of the origins of life?   **KU6**

Intermediate 2:
Can a Christian accept evolutionary theory? Give reasons for your answer.   **KU6**

Intermediate 1:
How does evolutionary theory explain the origin and development of life?   **KU4**

Homework

Prepare a short class presentation on your own views about the creation/evolution debate.

Personal Reflection

How can you make your life meaningful?

What Has This Course Been For?

The course has a number of broad aims:

◆ To help you understand how religious people, in particular those within Christianity explain some of life's big questions and to compare and contrast this with the answers given by scientific materialists.

◆ To help you explore three important areas:

– How humans come to understand the world around them.

– What different views there are about the origin of the Universe.

– What different views there are about the origin of human life.

◆ To help you consider your own response to these issues of belief.

◆ To assist you in developing your own sense of meaning, value and purpose in life through learning about and reflecting upon the beliefs of others in relation to these big questions.

Throughout all of this, it is hoped that you will explore your own views of each topic and come to your own conclusions about each of the areas you will explore. Beyond that, this might change the way you think about things and so what you do. Perhaps this will lead to you changing the world. RMPS is more than just *learning about*, it is *learning from*. This course should help you to consider your own responses to some of the biggest issues of belief around today through reflecting upon the various viewpoints covered in the course.

How Can I Decide?

The issues in this book are very complex and even people who have spent their lives studying them don't always agree. People can study these topics in depth for many years and still not know what the 'answer' is. The same people can change their opinions on the topics based on reason, argument, or a different understanding of a viewpoint or in light of new evidence. What is important is that people continue to look into these topics and discuss them. Only then might we eventually get closer to the truth, or at least how we should respond to the issue. These are sometimes complex issues which demand a fairly high level of understanding of theological, philosophical and scientific matters. However, it's all part of your learning journey and you shouldn't expect to have reached unchangeable conclusions at the end of this course. Learning is a lifelong journey after all. Hopefully what you have studied will help you to contribute to the debate and discussion and get a clearer idea of what you think and why you think it.

Learning Outcomes

There are slight differences between Intermediate 1, 2 and Higher. Make sure your teacher has the latest arrangements documents from the SQA or check them yourself at www.sqa.org.uk.

NB There is **NO** topic called *Christianity: Belief and Science* at Intermediate 1. However, the topics in this book also cover the Intermediate 1 unit: *Existence of God*. The additional topic of the *Problem of Evil* is also included in this book (Chapter 8).

SQA Course Arrangements

Please make sure your teacher checks this and is working from the latest arrangements, which can be found out at www.sqa.org.uk.

Intermediate 1 (NB = Existence of God Unit)

Outcome 1

Demonstrate knowledge and understanding of classical philosophical arguments.

Performance Criteria

a) Describe specific religious beliefs which are relevant to the question of the existence and nature of God.

b) Describe specific classical philosophical arguments which are cited in support of these beliefs.

Outcome 2

Explain objections to classical philosophical arguments.

Performance Criteria

a) Describe objections to specific classical philosophical arguments which are relevant to the question of the existence and nature of God.

b) Explain the reasons for these objections.

Outcome 3

Express a reasoned opinion about replies to objections to classical philosophical arguments.

Performance Criteria

a) Describe replies to objections to specific classical philosophical arguments which are relevant to the question of the existence and nature of God.

b) State opinions about the success of these replies in supporting the arguments.

c) Give reasons to support the opinions stated.

Intermediate 2

Outcome 1

Demonstrate knowledge and understanding of the nature of Christian revelation and scientific enquiry.

Performance Criteria

a) Describe the nature and importance of revelation in the Christian tradition.

b) Describe the methods of scientific enquiry.

c) Describe answers to specific questions about human origins which arise from Christian revelation and scientific enquiry.

Outcome 2

Compare and contrast interpretations of answers to important questions about human origins.

Performance Criteria

a) Describe interpretations of specific answers which suggest a conflict between Christian belief and scientific theory.

b) Describe interpretations of these answers which suggest that Christian belief and scientific theory are compatible.

c) Give reasons which explain the differences in these interpretations.

Outcome 3

Justify conclusions about interpretations of answers to important questions about human origins.

Performance Criteria

a) Explain perceived strengths and weaknesses of interpretations which suggest a conflict between Christian belief and scientific theory.

b) Explain perceived strengths and weaknesses of interpretations which suggest that Christian belief and scientific theory are compatible.

c) State opinions about the success of these interpretations in addressing the issues raised by scientific theory.

d) Give reasons to support the stated opinions.

Higher

Outcome 1

Demonstrate knowledge and understanding of the nature of Christian revelation and scientific enquiry.

Performance Criteria

a) Describe the nature and importance of revelation in the Christian tradition.

b) Describe the methods of scientific enquiry.

c) Describe answers to specific questions about human origins which arise from Christian revelation and scientific enquiry.

Outcome 2

Analyse interpretations of answers to important questions about human origins.

Performance Criteria

a) Explain interpretations of specific answers which suggest a conflict between Christian belief and scientific theory.

b) Explain interpretations of these answers which suggest that Christian belief and scientific theory are compatible.

c) Explain the reasons for differences between these interpretations.

Outcome 3

Evaluate interpretations of answers to important questions about human origins.

Performance Criteria

a) Explain perceived strengths and weaknesses of interpretations which suggest conflict between Christian belief and scientific theory.

b) Explain perceived strengths and weaknesses of interpretations which suggest that Christian belief and scientific theory are compatible.

c) Assess the implications of these interpretations for human understanding of the purpose and goals of life.

d) Give reasons to support the assessment made.

(*Source: www.sqa.org.uk*)

Description to Analysis

There is a 'pecking order' of skills you have to demonstrate in this course from the simplest which is stating a fact or opinion to the most complex which is assessing a viewpoint or analyzing an issue. In this unit, you are expected to be able to demonstrate knowledge and understanding of the facts, the viewpoints and the relationship between religious belief and the alternative/contradictory/complementary scientific theories. You are also supposed to be able to analyse and evaluate all of these – expressing your own view too on occasion. You must always do this in a reasonable way and supporting your answers with evidence wherever you can. It's easy in these topics just to give your opinion or to criticise someone else's, but you must make sure that you do so with supporting reasons which justify your opinion or criticism. The balance of this KU to AE varies according to your level of study.

The split of marks in the **Unit Assessments** (NABs to you) reflects this idea as follows:

NABs Marks split	Knowledge and Understanding	Analysis and Evaluation
Intermediate 1	70%	30%
Intermediate 2	60%	40%
Higher	60%	40%

In the **final exam**, the split is like this:

NABs Marks split	Knowledge and Understanding	Analysis and Evaluation
Intermediate 1	60%	40%
Intermediate 2	50%	50%
Higher	50%	50%

As for the exam, by the time you've read this book there should be a few past papers for you to look at. Your teacher will have a Specimen Exam Paper from the SQA. This will help them to make up the prelim and give you an idea of what the actual exam might be like. You should look at the SQA website too, because the nice people there have very helpfully put some past exam papers on the site with the marking instructions that the markers use (and these are the people who'll be marking your exam after all). There's also a thing called the SQA Standards website – remind your teacher about this one!

Sample Assessment Questions with Sample Answers

Here are three sample assessment questions with three sample answer structures. These are in note form to give you an idea of the kind of thing which should be included in a good answer. In the exam you should write your answers in prose, but doing a note form plan is always a good idea. Remember that how clearly you express yourself does matter. The NAB questions aren't significantly different from the exam questions in style so we can use these for practice for both. Remember that your NABs are also practice for the final exam! (Although the actual questions will be different, of course.)

Intermediate 1

When a religious person looks at the world and sees suffering and evil, at least he knows that the Free Will Defence argument can make sense of it.

Do you agree? Give **two** reasons for your answer.   **AE8**

Structure of Answer

◆ Explain the Freewill Defence argument = evil and suffering need to happen because humans need to be free to behave as they like and the consequences have to happen to safeguard free will.   **(AE2)**

◆ Agree because God give humans free will so they are not robots but free beings.   **(AE2)**

◆ Agree because free will built into the system – unfortunately leads to negative consequences sometimes but we have to accept that.   **(AE2)**

◆ Disagree because it isn't much of a comfort to someone who is suffering that they are only doing so to safeguard the idea of Free will.   **(AE2)**

◆ Disagree because a lot of evil and suffering is caused by natural evil which God could deal with without having any effect on human free will.   **(AE2)**

Intermediate 2

Can a Christian accept Darwin's theory of evolution and still remain a Christian?

Give reasons for your answer.   **AE10**

Structure of Answer

◆ Outline Darwin's/Neo-Darwinian theories of evolution = random mutations lead to survival advantages in particular environments – lead to increased likelihood of passing on the advantageous genes to offspring and so = evolution by natural selection.   **(AE2/3)**

◆ Explain that Christian teaching about the origin of life based on belief that life on Earth originated from God – can refer to a Bible story either literally or symbolically understood.   **(AE1/2)**

◆ Discuss the view that evolution completely opposes creation by God (give evidence e.g. fossils, genetic relationships, vestigial organs etc.) and therefore Christians cannot accept evolutionary theory without abandoning religious beliefs. Explain that evolutionary theory based on scientific method and that evidence contradicts religious belief. You may want to add a brief comment about the claims of Intelligent Design.   **(AE3/4)**

◆ Discuss the view that evolution can be considered as the mechanism through which God created life on Earth and therefore is compatible with creation of life by God. Can discuss the idea that evolution explains the physical origin and development of life whereas Christian views cover the meaning and purpose of life.   **(AE3/4)**

◆ For each of the AE points above it is wise to include at least one quotation from each supporting your line of argument. **(AE1/2)**

◆ A concluding sentence or two is always a good way to finish a question like this, summarising whether you agree with the statement or not. **(AE1/2)**

Higher

A Christian must accept Genesis 1 as literally true. Do you agree? Give reasons for your answer. **AE10**

Structure of Answer

◆ Explain what is meant by literally true in relation to a brief outline of the story i.e. that the creation of the Universe happened exactly as the Bible says it did – in six days of 24 hours, for example. **(AE1/2)**

◆ Explain that Christians must accept this literalism because the Bible says so, therefore we have to accept the truth of the story. **(AE1/2)** If we start choosing some things as literal and others as symbolic then we might end up not believing in any of the Bible. **(AE1/2)** Explain that even though the literal story might seem unlikely, Christianity is based on faith and so a believer should accept the story in faith at face value. **(AE1/2)** You might support this belief with the further belief that the nature of God means that the creation could have taken place exactly the way the Bible describes it. **(AE1/2)**

◆ Explain that some Christians see no need to interpret the story literally and see accepting it as symbolism does not show a lack of faith at all (quite the opposite). **(AE1/2)** A symbolic interpretation means that you can accept that God created the Universe but not that he did it according to the simple story in Genesis. **(AE1/2)** Explain further that the Genesis story is not intended as a science textbook **(AE1)** and that the story is a meaningful way to express the message and importance of creation as opposed to the scientific principles behind it. **(AE1/2)**

◆ Concluding section summarising your views on whether you agree with the statement or not. **(AE1/2)**

INDEX